Jason Robertson is a pseudonym for the director of personnel of a *Fortune*-100-rated company. He holds a B.S. in Business Administration from the University of Connecticut and has over 20 years personnel management experience with both government and industry. He is the author of several professional articles, among them "Recruiting Today's Sales Professional" and "How Do you Say 'Help Wanted'?" He also conducts seminars on the subject of recruiting, interviewing, and hiring for the professional development of managers.

How to WIN in a JOB INTERVIEW

Jason Robertson

A SPECTRUM BOOK

Prentice-Hall, Inc., *Englewood Cliffs, New Jersey 07632*

Library of Congress Cataloging in Publication Data

Robertson, Jason.
   How to win in a job interview.

   (A Spectrum Book)
   Includes index.
   1. Employment interviewing. I. Title.
HF5549.5.I6R6   650'.14   78-7569
ISBN 0-13-439521-2
ISBN 0-13-439513-1 pbk.

For my wife, Susan

Printed in the United States of America

10 9 8 7 6 5

PRENTICE-HALL INTERNATIONAL, INC., *London*
PRENTICE-HALL OF AUSTRALIA PTY. LIMITED, *Sydney*
PRENTICE-HALL OF CANADA, LTD., *Toronto*
PRENTICE-HALL OF INDIA PRIVATE LIMITED, *New Delhi*
PRENTICE-HALL OF JAPAN, INC., *Tokyo*
PRENTICE-HALL OF SOUTHEAST ASIA PTE. LTD., *Singapore*
WHITEHALL BOOKS LIMITED, *Wellington, New Zealand*

CONTENTS

PREFACE

The face-to-face interview has become an almost universal selection tool in hiring people. As with any technique or practice, there are certain "tricks of the trade." The professional interviewer acquires these tricks by undergoing extensive training and by day-to-day, on-the-job practice; but you only interview occasionally, so you're at a disadvantage. However, once you understand what's happening to you in an interview, you can get *off* the defensive and be chosen for the job you want. You'll learn how in the chapters that follow.

Introduction

Why you're losing out

You're looking for a job? Welcome to the club. At one time or another, most of us have either been out of work or looking for something better. Maybe you want to land that first job. Or you need to get out of a dead-end position. It could be that there's been a reorganization in your company or you have a personality conflict with your boss. Whatever the reason, you're either laid off, fired, or frustrated in your present job.

If you've been reading the want ads and calling friends who might help you, you realize that finding a new job or jumping to a better one is not going to be easy. You're becoming frustrated; you seem to be using up more time than you can afford, and you're beginning to feel like a piece of picked-over meat in the supermarket.

You've probably prepared résumés that outline your education and past employment experience. You've regis-

1

tered with employment agencies and read and responded to as many newspaper want ads as you can get your hands on. You've sought advice and help from friends, relatives, and business acquaintances. You've written letters and submitted résumés. You've learned to bring along a paperback book to read while you wait in line at the local unemployment office. You've called on companies, hoping to talk to someone in charge of employment. You've spent a lot of time and effort trying to get that all-important invitation that says: "We're interested in talking to you. Please come in for an interview."

You go in; the interview seems to run all right. When it's over, you shake hands with the interviewer, go home, and wait. Several anxious days, sometimes weeks, pass. Finally a letter comes in the mail. You are thanked for your interest and promised that your résumé will be kept on file. Rejection. Why? What caused you to lose out? If you got as far as an interview, then you have to assume that you were probably rejected on the basis of what happened during the interview.

Surprised? You shouldn't be. The interview has become the crucial part of the employment process; frequently, it's the one area least understood by you—the job seeker. Sure, you may have spent weeks carefully preparing a résumé, reading ads, and writing letters. But when you finally got that interview, how thoroughly had you prepared for that all-important, face-to-face meeting with your prospective employer?

"But," you might say, "how do I prepare for an interview?"

It's not surprising that you'd ask. A lot of material has been written for the professional interviewer, but practically nothing to help the person being interviewed.

There's no way for you to receive a formal training program on interviewing, the kind your interviewer has probably been through. The professional interviewer has been trained to gain better insight into you, the applicant. And now you can gain insight, too. I'm going to make you aware of what's taking place during the interview. You'll never have to wonder again about how you "did." You'll know.

In short, I'm going to reveal how the interview process works, so that you won't be burned again. I've seen too many promising candidates, who have sat across from me, fail to win the job they really wanted. Why? Because they couldn't beat the system that my fellow personnel people and I have set up. Why should I, a professional interviewer, extend a helping hand like this? I've got two reasons: The first is altruistic, and the second is purely mercenary. Let's talk about the first.

With the economic climate the way it is, it's getting increasingly tougher to break into the good jobs. You know what I'm talking about: a nice salary, a solid company, job satisfaction, and promotional opportunities. I've met and heard about people with potential who were washed out, because they couldn't demonstrate their ability during a job interview. In most instances, they never knew why they didn't get the job. It's time to give these people a break; and if you happen to be one of them, congratulations. You've bought the right book.

That brings me to reason number two. I like the good life and enjoy the fruits of my labor. The knowledge I've picked up over the years is valuable. You have purchased many years of experience boiled down to a few hours of reading. I benefit from your purchase, and you benefit from my experience.

The following chapters are succinct and to the point. You shouldn't have to wade through a lot of verbiage to get at the information you'll need. I suggest you read this book all the way through once, marking passages that seem particularly pertinent to your situation. Then reread the passages you've marked before going out on your next interview. Once you understand the subtleties involved in the interview process, you'll stand a better chance of winning in the job interview.

1

Some things you may have overlooked

Before we get into interview strategy and how you should deal with it, we need to talk about some basics. Failure to take care of the following may knock you out of the box.

Will you get to the interview on time?

Do you know how to get to the interview? Will you keep the interviewer(s) waiting? It is extremely important for you to get to the interview on time. Your prospective employer will have planned your visit well in advance and will have set up a schedule for you. Usually, several interviews will be required; so your visit will have been coordinated with several company representatives. If you arrive late, you run the risk of affecting several people with your tardiness.

Very often, large companies have several operating subsidiaries in the same geographical area. If you are not aware of the specific subsidiary or the specific department, you can get lost. For example, a major company I know of has five operating businesses in one city. Each company has its own employment department; but all five companies are listed under one name in the telephone directory, with different telephone numbers for each operating company. About the only way you can find the exact company where you will be interviewed is by obtaining the exact address and specific instructions regarding building name or number, floor, room, and so on. To do less may result in your becoming lost, and as a result, late. Don't take chances, call the company beforehand, and get detailed, specific instructions as to when and where the interview will take place.

Will you look presentable?

Maybe your wife thinks the red and blue checked sports jacket she bought you is the latest word in fashion, but it is doubtful that many employers will be that impressed with it. Sure, your husband likes you in slacks; but leave them at home, and wear a modest but stylish dress to your job interview. Judgments based on first impressions are wrong, unfair, and practically criminal. But let's be honest. We're all human, and consciously or unconsciously, we make them. So at least until you are hired, stay in the mainstream with what you wear.

Most interviewers will look at the clothes you wear and how you wear them. Furthermore, most interviewers will evaluate you on your appearance, and this will generally include grooming as well as attire. My advice is to present a neat appearance that conveys a businesslike attitude and that you believe will conform to the particular mode of dress prevalent in the company interviewing you. Regardless of how well you are evaluated based on your academic credentials, work experience, career objectives, and overall capabilities, your presenting a neat appearance during the first, important meeting can be very helpful in creating a favorable interview climate.

Did you research the company interviewing you?

When the receptionist shows you to a chair and tells you to wait, don't dig out the crossword puzzle you've been doing. Instead, pick up the company publication in the waiting area, and learn about the firm. Find out as much as you can. How big is the company? What does it make or sell? Is it expanding? Is it profitable? Unless you know something about the company or division, you won't be able to deal with the interviewer in his or her world. And it will be more difficult to determine whether or not the company is right for you.

You can gather a lot of information about the company beforehand by researching it in your local library. There are several publications—such as *Moody's Industrial Manual, Standard & Poor's Register, Fortune Magazine,* and *Business Week*—that will provide you with a good idea of what the company is all about. Another possible source of information is the annual report, if the company publishes one. The annual report can be obtained free of charge from the company itself. Other sources of information are friends, relatives, or acquaintances who already work there. Go ahead and pick their brains. You can also phone the firm's public relations department and ask them to tell you about the company and to mail you literature about it. Most companies are willing to do this for you. They are concerned about their public image and their community relations.

Once you gather such information and absorb it, you will be able to interact more effectively during the interview. You will have confidence and be better able to understand the interviewer's role in the company, and you will be able to ask more relevant questions during the interview.

Are you a good listener?

Too many applicants have lost out simply because they were poor listeners. I recall one fellow who seemed to think that everything I said called for acknowledgment on his part. I never got to finish a sentence.

"So you fish," I said to Bertram (not his name). "So do I. The season. . . ."

"Fishing, yes," Bertram said. "I've got all the equipment, make my own flies; of course my wife, she hates to clean anything I've caught. . . ." Bertram got a polite handshake at the end of the interview and was told we'd "be in touch."

Let me give you some ideas on listening. Research has shown that although everyone listens, most of us listen ineffectively. If we understand what the essential elements are that make some people good listeners and others poor ones, then we can learn how to increase our ability to identify and retain the critical content of what we hear.

To be a good, active listener, you must recognize and grasp several components of listening skills. To begin with, you must prepare to listen. This is accomplished by recalling everything you know that relates to what you are about to hear. Let's see how this process works. Imagine that you're about to hear an interviewer describe the organization of the company to you. You would go over in your mind everything you know about organizations. Starting at the top, you might think, "Oh yes, let me see; I know something about the chairman of the board, the board of directors, the chief operating executive or the president, staff functions, vice-presidents, directors; various departments such as finance, public relations, sales, marketing, personnel, legal. I know about line and staff, . . ."

As you warm up this way for listening to what the speaker is about to say, be prepared to look for similarities or differences between what you already know and what you're about to hear. You prepare yourself by asking the general question, "What do I already know?" Then you ask yourself about the relationships and the similarities and/or differences between what you know and what you hear as you listen.

You also must be able to summarize what the speaker has said. This can be accomplished by recognizing the speaker's main points and the supporting statements he or she uses to embellish them. For example, the speaker may say, "A requirement of this position is extensive travel away from home." The main point is "extensive travel." The speaker may then support that point by saying, "Most of the travel is of short duration and only requires one or two days away at a time. Also, the travel is mainly to our manufacturing plant in Peoria, so the trips are easy." The main point is "extensive travel," the supporting points are "short duration," "two days away," and "Peoria." In order to listen actively, you must be able to identify the main points and supporting points while you are listening. By doing so, you will retain more of the statement.

To summarize a statement effectively, it is extremely helpful to note only those words and phrases that are important in identifying the main points and the supporting points. These words can be called "key words," as they provide the key to what the speaker is trying to get across. For example, in the statement, "This position requires a recent degree in computer science," the key word is "recent." If your degree is ten years old, you may not be the ideal candidate for whatever opening the speaker is describing. Recognition of the key word, *recent*, will assist you in listening to the speaker's main point, which is "recent degree."

In supporting the main point, the speaker may say, "We have recently leased a fourth-generation computer, and we have had a skills obsolescence problem with our current staff." Here the key phrases are "fourth-generation computer" and "skills obsolescence." They are used to support the main point of finding a candidate with a "recent degree."

As the speaker talks, in addition to identifying main and supporting points, you must also be able to group the points into such categories as similarities/differences and advantages/disadvantages. In the above situation, you might ask yourself, "How is my background similar or different in terms of the requirements for the job? Is it an advantage or disadvantage to work with fourth-generation equipment?" As you categorize the main and supporting points and compare your own situation against them, you are well on your way to becoming a good, interactive listener. You are now in a position to ask the speaker to clarify statements for you or to elaborate on them and also to confirm your understanding of any statement that isn't clear.

The final key to good listening is to be able to overcome any blocks that may be present that will distract you. Blocks to effective listening can be environmental distraction such as sights and sounds, personal opinions or prejudices that prevent you from identifying the speaker's entire message, accents, improper grammar or slang that forces your attention to the structures rather than the content and meaning, and finally, selective listening—where you only allow yourself to hear what you want to hear and selectively tune out everything else.

Here are some additional do's and don't's when it comes to listening: Recognize the fact that you think about four times as fast as a person can talk. Don't use that excess time to turn your thoughts elsewhere.

Do not let certain words, phrases, or ideas prejudice you against the speaker so that you cannot listen objectively to what is being said.

If you are annoyed or irritated by what has been said, do not interrupt the speaker and try to straighten it out either in your own mind or verbally.

Do not tune out if you feel that it will take too much time and effort to understand something. Do not deliberately turn your thoughts to other subjects if you believe the speaker has nothing interesting to say.

Do not let a person's appearance or speech pattern influence you into thinking that he or she may not have anything worthwhile to say.

Do not act as if you are listening to someone if you are not. Pay attention!

Remember, good listening is essential in an interview;

and further, because of human nature, most people like good listeners. It's a fact. People prefer to have people listen to them much more than they prefer to listen themselves. My last question in this chapter is a loaded one.

Did you know where the interviewer was "coming from?"

I admit to this being a loaded question, because if you haven't read the book, you won't know the answer. Let me explain. Most interviewers try to conduct an interview in four steps:

1. Getting started
2. Getting facts and insights
3. Stimulating your interest
4. Closing the interview

Getting started

To get started, the interviewer will encourage you to talk freely. He or she will do this by putting you at ease and maintaining a comfortable atmosphere. The more comfortable you are, the more likely you are to open up. I have two words for you at this point.

"Watch out!"

Don't get taken in and reveal your innermost thoughts. Go ahead! Be warm and friendly, but practice restraint. This is no time for open confession.

Getting facts and insights

Here the interviewer will delve into your previous employment, will try to pin down dates, ask you why you left each job, and uncover your career objectives. You do have career objectives, don't you? If not, take time out now to think about them. They are as important as references. Once you've formulated your objectives in your mind, jot them down on a piece of paper and commit them to memory. If you can't convince a professional interviewer you're going somewhere, you'll never get the opportunity to get there.

The interviewer may also ask you about your educational background, periods of unemployment—if any—and the names and titles of your previous supervisors so that reference checks can be made. The interviewer will take notes of this key information.

The interviewer will try to maintain control of the interview by searching for satisfactory answers, using follow-up questions, exploring superficial responses, and encouraging you to talk. Remember: The interviewer is "buying," and you are "selling." And nine times out of ten, it's a buyer's market.

Stimulating your interest

To stimulate your interest, the interviewer will probably explain the job to you; describe the company, and encourage you to ask questions. He or she will avoid revealing any desirable characteristics being sought in the prospective employee, will attempt to answer all your questions, and will avoid overselling the position.

13

Closing the interview

To close the interview, most interviewers summarize the main points brought out during the exchange. They will avoid making a commitment to you and will not express any enthusiasm or raise your level of expectation. The interviewer will detail the next steps to be taken and express appreciation for your interest. In some situations, the interviewer may offer to pick up the tab for the interview trip; but don't expect to be reimbursed.

Now that we've covered some of the basics, we can get into the interview process.

2

Finding your way through the hiring maze

If we could diagram the sequence most companies follow when hiring, it would look like the chart on the following page.

Screening the paperwork

First, companies gather as many applications as they can, usually by placing newspaper ads, listing the job with employment agencies, or by utilizing search firms. This results in an influx of résumés and applications. The recruiter, usually someone from the personnel department, prescreens against a background of specific requirements for the position. The company has examined its needs and has developed a hiring plan for filling the opening. This plan spells out in detail the specific educational background needed; the experience required; the personal traits and characteristics necessary for success on the job.

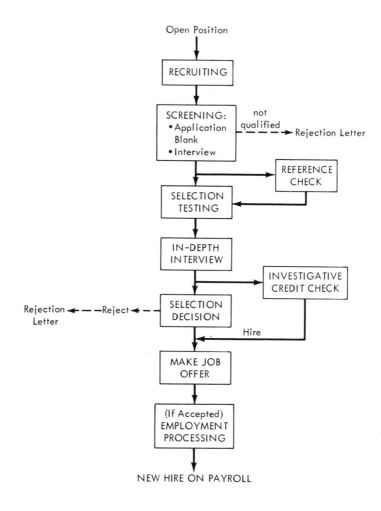

Who gets interviewed?

After the paperwork is screened, the recruiter frequently finds that he or she can sort the résumés into three categories. The first category of applicants doesn't come close to the hiring plan and are rejects. They usually get a form letter telling them that their "credentials will be preserved for future reference" and "should a position become available which would use [their] particular experience to its best advantage, [they] will be contacted." The second category of applicants meets part of the hiring plan but are not exceptional. The third category is for the promising; hopefully, that category contains the résumé of the applicant who will eventually get the job. Applicants who make it past this initial paperwork screening are invited in for a screening interview.

The initial screening interview

The screening interview allows a recruiter or a team of recruiters to see a large number of applicants in a comparatively short period of time. Usually, a screening interview lasts about a half-hour. Most companies generally schedule candidates at forty-five-minute intervals. During that period, they seek specific information on each candidate.

The main purpose is to screen out, in as short an interview as possible, applicants who obviously lack the necessary job qualifications. It also provides another interviewer's evaluation if two interviewers are conducting the screenings. Before inviting you in for a screening interview, interviewers will have analyzed your paper work, so that they can organize their thoughts and familiarize themselves with your background and experience.

Three strikes and you're out

You should be aware of three items an interviewer will most likely look at before talking to you. We call them (1) "knockout" items, (2) "concern" items, and (3) "incomplete" items. All positions have certain, minimum requirements that automatically exclude some applicants. These are called "knockout" factors. Some knockout factors that can be gleaned from the application form are:

- Lack of experience or training
- Job-related health problems
- Unavailability to start employment within a reasonable period of time
- Unrealistic salary expectations

The second group of items that will alert an interviewer are "concern" items. Once a recruiter spots a "concern" item, he or she will become cautious about pursuing you as an applicant. Some typical "concern" items are:

- Periods of unemployment. (Why?)
- Questionable reasons for leaving previous jobs. (Is there a pattern? Are you a job hopper?)
- Unusual salary progression. (How has your salary progressed in relation to others in the same career field or line of work?)
- Failure to account for all time periods. (Do your dates con-

flict with one another, or are they incomplete on your application?)

- Time lapses in educational programs. (Was there a break in your education? Why is it incomplete? Did it take you longer than usual to get your high school diploma or degree? If so, why?)

The interviewer, in looking over your paper work, makes notes directly on your application blank or résumé. These notes will serve as a reminder of the "concern" items that will be explored during the screening interview.

The third category of items an interviewer looks for before the screening interview can be labeled "incomplete" items. All of the information requested on an employment application is important. If you overlook a major portion of the application blank, chances are the interviewer will ask you to write in the missing information before you start the interview. Or, if it's only one or two questions, you may be asked to fill in the information during the interview.

How you'll be rated

During the initial screening interview, the interviewer will most likely rate you for several selection factors. These will differ from company to company and job to job. Generally, you'll be screened for such characteristics as:

- Aggressiveness and enthusiasm
- Responsibility and maturity
- Intellectual ability and communication skills
- Personal relations

At the conclusion of the interview, the interviewer will submit comments on the likelihood of your success to the next person in the hiring sequence.

Conclusion of the screening interview

At the end of the screening interview, the interviewer will recommend whether or not you should be pursued as a job candidate. At this point, the interviewer can make a decision to test you or line you up for a second, in-depth interview, commonly referred to as a "selection interview." Or the interviewer can make a decision to reject you.

Even though you may want to know where you stand at the end of an interview, even if you're to be rejected, you most likely will not be given a verbal turn-down. Most companies have found that such a rejection after a screening interview can lead to anything from discrimination complaints to lawsuits. So don't expect this kind of feedback from your company interviewer. It's only natural to wonder why you've been rejected. However, only the most skilled interviewer can walk that tightrope and provide you with a response general enough to avoid specific reasons for rejection, specific enough yet one that will satisfy you. So, if rejected, you'll probably get a letter in the mail. But enough gloom. Let's say the recruiter does have an interest in you; then you'll be invited for a second interview, or you may be given employment tests. Either one of these actions is a positive sign; they indicate you're a definite contender for the job. The field has narrowed, and you are one of the finalists. From now on, the interviews will be longer, tougher, and more in-depth. But relax; the chapters that follow will help you to win!

3

The interviewer goes to work on you

As soon as you sit down in the interviewer's office, you're fair game. That's right. The interviewer will be working on you with two objectives in mind: (1) to establish a trusting relationship, and (2) to gain facts about you. The reason for the first objective is to create at atmosphere in which you'll want to open up, so the interviewer will have an easier time achieving the second objective.

Most applicants will only reveal about 20 percent of themselves; the other 80 percent will remain below the surface. Don't expect the interviewer to take your responses at face value; chances are, he or she will be too aware for that. What the interviewer will be doing is continuously making and testing assumptions about you. This is one of the most important techniques used in interviewing. It's frequently called *hypothesis testing*. Here's how it works. The interviewer formulates a hypothesis about you. It can be based on something in your résumé or something on your application or something you may have said.

Let's assume that you're applying for an administrative position that requires a great deal of contact with people outside the firm. Further, as part of your job, you will have to put pressure on these people in order to get results. The interviewer may formulate a hypothesis that says, "This candidate does not like to contact outside people; further, this candidate is too shy to exert the pressure needed to be successful in this position."

Now, then, the interviewer will construct an entire line of questions, the answers to which will provide the evidence to support or deny the hypothesis. The interviewer will come at you from every angle with questions dealing with your attitude, ability, experience, and desire to perform the task of contacting outside people. Hypothesis testing can, and usually does, form the basis for all questions that are asked during an interview. It is widely used, because the concept is sound and because it facilitates the direction and scope of questioning. Once the interviewer assumes a condition or forms a hypothesis about anything, then it becomes a relatively minor chore to bombard an applicant with questions. On the surface, you may not know what's going on; but if you understand this concept, then you'll be able to recognize what's behind the interviewer's line of questioning.

Let me give you another example. Frequently, I've encountered female college graduates applying for secretarial positions. Because professional positions are scarce, these applicants believe they should compromise their goals, take a crash course in steno and typing, and position themselves as secretaries. But, I for one don't like to place any college graduates in nonprofessional jobs. First of all, the Equal Employment Opportunity Commission takes a dim view of companies that have qualified women in positions lower than equally qualified males. Secondly, once such a graduate is hired as a secretary, she soon becomes bored with the work and becomes a morale problem or a turnover problem. Whenever a college graduate applies for a secretarial position, my immediate hypothesis is that she's looking for a way to get her foot in the door until something better comes along. To prove or disprove that hypothesis, I'll ask her questions dealing with short- and long-term career objectives, salary expectations, job challenge, capacity for routine and repetitious tasks, tolerance for working under people who may not be as bright as she. Finally, I'll probe for the motivation behind her seeking a lower-level position than she appears capable of handling. If she answers all my questions in a manner that leaves no doubt in my mind that she really wants to be a secretary and nothing else, then I'd probably hire her. If, however, I get a clue that indicates otherwise, she'll be rejected. To hire her would only result in disappointment and disillusionment further down the road if and when that better job doesn't materialize.

When you sense a line of questioning that focuses on one or two specific areas in your background, experience, or qualifications, you'll know that the interviewer has assumed something about you and that he or she is trying to prove or disprove that assumption or hypothesis. Armed with this knowledge, you should be sure that your answers to any and all questions support your objective!

The interviewer will work on getting the facts

During the interview, a tremendous amount of information will be exchanged. The interviewer will be confronted with trying to separate fact from fiction. The ease with which this can be accomplished depends on how much information you provide on a certain subject and how much of that information is real or made up. If there's reality in a statement, then it's a statement of fact. It can be observed, it's certain, and it can be proven. If, on the other hand, you leave something open to interpretation on the part of the interviewer, then it's an inference. It was not certain, and it could not be proven. Before the interviewer can move from inferences to facts, he or she has to make assumptions. This means that the interviewer will try to get more and more information regarding particular data about you and gradually will move from the inference level to the fact level. Let me show you how this works.

Let's say your résumé lists three colleges in six years. The interviewer could infer that you flunked out of the first two schools and finally ended up at a collegiate "country club." So, he or she will check this out by asking you questions. Perhaps in your freshman year, you came down with mononucleosis and had to drop out. When you went back to college, you chose a school closer to home. Then your father got transferred to the west coast; and when your family moved, you did, too. Your third college was a small liberal arts school in California. Despite setbacks, you persevered and got that diploma. What's the point? Just this: The interviewer didn't know the facts pertaining to the three colleges listed on your résumé. If he or she had inferred that you flunked out of two schools, it would have been to your disadvantage. On the other hand, by revealing the true circumstances behind your attending three colleges, you have alerted the interviewer to a strength, instead of uncovering a weakness. That strength is the perseverance you exhibited in getting your degree.

Be prepared to deal with any weaknesses in

background. Turn them into strengths. I'll have more to say about this technique later. Also, if you feel that the interviewer can or does infer anything negative in any information that you provide, you must ensure that you clear it up and leave very little doubt as to what the true facts are. Interviewers know that their own perceptions of you will be distorted. They also know that it's difficult to obtain an accurate insight and analysis of anyone in a short period of time. They will listen carefully to every word you're saying, then interpret that information as they separate the facts from the insights. In order to do this and to acquire the kind of information needed, interviewers have to ask questions. And that leads us into the subject of questioning techniques.

Questioning techniques

Interviewers know that using the right kind of questioning pays off in obtaining information. They also realize that there are "two" applicants present during the interview: One is the real you; the other is the applicant as you present yourself. Of course, you want to show yourself in the most favorable light or at least as you'd like the interviewer to see you. It's the interviewer's job to distinguish between the real and the make-believe. Good questioning techniques help to make that distinction.

First let's look at what interviewers *won't* do. In most cases, the interviewer will not ask questions that reveal his or her own attitudes, such as:

- "That was a good reason to change jobs."
- "I thought you did a good job. How do you feel about it?"

- "What's been your experience in dealing with troublemakers who review your expense statements?"

Nor will they ask questions already answered on the application form or résumé. This serves no purpose and is a waste of valuable time. Also, the interviewer will not ask questions that are not related to the task at hand, such as:

- "What did you think of the ball game last night?"
- "How has the weather been out your way?"

Basically, there are two types of questions you need to know about: the "direct" question and the "open-ended" question. The direct question is a question that can be answered adequately in a few words. For example:

- "How long have you worked for your present supervisor?"
- "What was your favorite course in college?"
- "How many people work out of your office?"

The open-ended question, on the other hand, is one that usually requires more than a few words for an adequate response. This type of question is designed to give you, the applicant, lots of room in answering; it is also used to get the applicant to open up. Some open-ended questions are:

- "Would you tell me about your present job?"
- "How would you describe yourself?"
- "What do you feel are your supervisor's strengths?"

Both types of questions have their place in an interview. The interviewer will use direct questions to draw out specific information; however, heavy reliance on them can turn the interview into an interrogation and may cause you to become defensive. Here's a tip: If the interviewer uses a lot of direct questions, you should be able to anticipate the line of questioning. When this happens, you'll have lead time to formulate acceptable answers.

In most situations, the interviewer probing for information regarding your attitudes, successes, failures, and the like will use open-ended questions. Open-ended questions allow you to express yourself freely. And they encourage you to do most of the talking. If the interviewer talks a third or more of the interviewing time, he or she is a poor interviewer. If you find yourself doing most of the talking, then you know you're in the hands of a pro.

Two other types of questions often used in an interview are "reflection" and "interpretation." The reflection question can be very effective. The interviewer repeats or rephrases a portion of what you have said. For example, suppose you say, "And then I began having disagreements with my boss." The interviewer will want to know more about these disagreements; so he or she will reflect your statement by saying, "You had disagreements with your boss?" Almost inevitably, you'll begin to talk in more detail about your disagreements with your boss. Reflection is used sparingly. Overuse of this technique can lend an air of absurdity to an interview. But when it's intermixed with other techniques, interviewers find it useful in getting information out of you.

"Interpretation" is a technique in which the interviewer goes beyond merely repeating what you say and attempts to interpret. He or she pieces together what you've said and then adds something to it, hoping to delve more deeply into the subject. The interviewer might say,

"Could it be that these disagreements with your supervisor resulted from your resentment of his promotion?" Be careful this technique doesn't catch you off guard and force you into a direct response. When this occurs, the interviewer can dig even deeper. If the interviewer is not highly skilled, rapport can be destroyed by "interpretation." This loss of rapport can hurt you more than the interviewer, so be on guard against making implications from which an interviewer can structure an interpretation.

So you'll know how to recognize "reflection" and "interpretation" when you hear them, here is an exchange from an actual job interview.

CANDIDATE: I am interested in joining your firm, because the opportunity for advancement is greater.

INTERVIEWER: You're looking for advancement?
(Reflection)

CANDIDATE: Yes. If I stayed longer, I'd probably do well where I am. But I hear that advancement is faster in your industry.

INTERVIEWER: Why do you feel that way?
(Open Ended)

CANDIDATE: Well, I've talked to several people, and they say that your company is the leader in a fast-growth industry.

INTERVIEWER: These people have convinced you that it's the best thing to do?
(Interpretation)

CANDIDATE: Yes, that's a fair way of putting it.

INTERVIEWER: Let's talk a little more about your present job. How are things going?
(Open Ended)

CANDIDATE: Things are going along fine. But I'm not moving as fast as I'd like to.

INTERVIEWER: You don't think you're moving fast enough?
(Reflection)

CANDIDATE: I have been doing okay. I do my work well. No complaints. But things could be much better in a way.

INTERVIEWER: Could you please explain?
(Open Ended)

CANDIDATE: Well, I like the company. They like me, and they give me plenty of responsibility. I like the people, but not the setup there.

INTERVIEWER: You don't like the setup?
(Reflection)

CANDIDATE: Too much firefighting, a lot of paper work, and no time to think. It makes you feel like you're on a merry-go-round and going no place.

INTERVIEWER: Would you say more about that?
(Open Ended)

CANDIDATE: I don't know. I thought of quitting, but that would have been foolish. Then I thought of your company.

INTERVIEWER: You mean that the idea of joining our company might have been triggered by your situation?

As you can see, the interviewer skillfully used various types of questions to get the applicant to open up. The final question was one of interpretation. The interviewer interpreted the candidate's reasons for wanting the position as having come about by accident rather than by design. The candidate has talked himself into a corner and is faced with the problem of talking his way out.

What's the message?—to recognize how a skillful interviewer can use various types of questions to get information out of you, information that may work to your disadvantage. To guard against that happening, you must learn to recognize where the interviewer is leading you with his or her line of questions. We talk about that next.

4

Controlling
the interview

The interviewer's one trump card is remaining in control. If you talk on and on, giving more detail than asked for, the interviewer will avoid using reinforcers like, "Mmhm, I see," and the like. If withholding reinforcers is not enough to make you stop talking, then you'll be interrupted. He or she will wait for a pause at the end of one of your sentences and then jump in with a neat transition such as, "Well, that tells me all I need to know about your educational background; now could we go on to discuss your work experience?" If that occurs, then you should pick up the cue and cut down on the length of your responses. If you're a nonstop talker who doesn't pause long enough, than you may be interrupted in midsentence. Don't let this happen! Let the interviewer maintain control. As long as you are aware of what is happening, you can adapt to the situation accordingly.

Up to this point we have discussed the use of the most commonly used questions: direct, open ended, reflective, and interpretative. We have also talked about how the interviewer will try to control the interview. Now, let's take a closer look at how a skilled interviewer uses these techniques to zero in on you and pinpoint the information sought from you.

Target: you

The professional interviewer conducts interviews with one objective in mind—to get factual information. For this reason, your responses to questions must meet certain criteria. For example, one criterion may call for clear, specific answers. If your responses are general, vague, or open to more than one interpretation, they're of questionable value. The interviewer will have to do more to ensure reaching a depth of understanding.

When your answers are vague

Perhaps the most basic technique used is a request for elaboration and clarification. Systematically, the subject area is explored in depth by probing into all aspects. The professional interviewer will skillfully dig in by using both open-ended questions and direct questions. In addition, he or she may occasionally use reflection or interpretation. These are excellent techniques, which by their nature request elaboration on your part. Now let me show you how the interviewer probes a candidate for elaboration and clarification:

INTERVIEWER: I'd be interested in knowing what's most important to you in a job.

CANDIDATE: Well, I think three things are important. First of
all, I think the job must present a challenge. Second, I feel
there must be opportunity for growth, both personally and
financially . . . and third, I'd like to have the opportunity to
become a manager of people in a short term.

INTERVIEWER: Would you explain what you care least about in a
job?

CANDIDATE: Sure. I don't like jobs where I'm unduly hampered
by policies and procedures.

INTERVIEWER: Oh, you feel that policies and procedures restrict
you as an employee?

CANDIDATE: Yes, to some extent.

INTERVIEWER: Would you explain that for me in more detail?

This brief exchange is indicative of what happens
when your answers prove vague. The interviewer's objective will be to explore all aspects in great depth and to
pursue the subject matter until enough information is
gathered to make a judgment. You may feel that "elaborating" and "clarifying" is threatening, that it might have a
negative influence on your level of participation; but this is
not always the case. You may regard it as an indication of
sincere interest and careful attention on the part of the
interviewer which will result in gaining greater respect
from you. If it does come across as threatening, try to
overcome your reaction calmly and confidently.

You should also be aware of several other techniques
that may be used on you in the in-depth interview. These
are "repeat questions," "looping back," "requesting
specifics," "exploring values and feelings," and "silence."
Let's take a closer look at these techniques.

Repeat questions are simply that. Answers to questions asked earlier in the interview did not satisfy the interviewer. Your response may be viewed as being evasive, superficial, or inconsistent. As the interview progresses, the interviewer may feel that he or she has won you over and that you now appear to be less threatened and more trusting. At this point, the interviewer may go back and ask the same question, hoping to get a better answer. This technique of repeating the same question is a good way for the interviewer to check out your answers to make sure you are consistent.

For example, I always look for the reasons behind people leaving jobs. I know from experience that people rarely leave a job for one single reason. Usually, when I ask why someone has left a job, I get one single reason. It could be for more money. It could be for more challenge. It could be for a promotion. It could be because of relocation of a spouse, and so forth. The one reason presented is usually one that sounds positive. By repeating my earlier questions later on in the interview when a better rapport has been established, I generally find out the real reasons. Several candidates who had left "for better opportunities" openly admitted later on in their interviews that they had been involuntarily terminated, or more bluntly, fired.

Be sure to be consistent in your answers throughout the interview. Don't drop your guard and provide contradictory information. Believe me, inconsistency works against you. This holds true for multiple interviews as well. If you give one interviewer one answer and a second interviewer a different answer, that inconsistency will work to your detriment. Formulate your responses beforehand

and stick to your story. Be alert for repeat questions, whether they are from the same interviewer or from successive interviewers.

Looping back

Looping back is a technique an interviewer uses when he or she senses you're holding back vital information. The more you're questioned, the more evasive you become. In that situation, the technique used by the interviewer may be to drop the line of questioning and return to it later . . . not by repeating the line of questioning verbatim, but by approaching the subject from a different direction. It is different from a repeat question in that the interviewer will attempt to get at the same information by using a completely different approach.

For example, you may have a gap in your employment record, and you may have filled it in by saying that you were a consultant during that period. The interviewer will question you about the kind of consulting you performed, who you consulted for, and so forth. In reality, you may have been unemployed and were consulting one or two days a month over a long time span. As the interviewer probes deeper and deeper into your activities as a consultant, you become more and more evasive. The interviewer will appear to drop the line of questioning and move on to another subject. Later on during the interview, you may be asked to provide your annual earnings as reported on your W-2 forms. If your earnings during your consulting period do not substantiate full-time consulting, the interviewer will have obtained his or her answer to previous questions by using a completely different approach.

Once again, be prepared to present consistent information that will hang together under all kinds of questioning techniques. Being aware of the "looping back" technique will enable you to recognize the motive behind seemingly innocent questions wherein the interviewer subtly returns to seeking vital information and hopefully catches you off guard.

Requesting Specifics

Another technique that may be used on you is that of requesting specific examples. For example, if you indicate a liking for assignments with considerable responsibility, you might be asked to describe the most responsible assignment you have had during the last six months. You should be prepared to render examples of any tasks or assignments that you point out to the interviewer. Further, you should be ready to answer specific questions that will be asked in connection with any examples you furnish. Try to support your example of a tough problem you solved during the past year. After you cite the example, you should be prepared to answer such specific questions as:

"Did you have any help in solving that problem?"

"What percentage of the work can be directly attributed to your efforts?"

"What recognition did you get for solving the problem?"

"Who else was recognized?"

"Was the solution accepted by your supervisor? Was it implemented? Was it a creative solution or an application of an existing solution?"

When you furnish an example, give one that truly represents your own work and not that of others. By doing so, you'll be able to answer any questions with a thorough knowledge and high degree of confidence. That knowledge and confidence will show through, and you'll rate highly in the interview.

Exploring values and feelings

Interviewers can gain considerable insight into your personality not only by exploring your accomplishments and background but by exploring your values and feelings as well. The experienced interviewer knows that some questions call for more or less factual information. These are called "objective questions." Other questions key in on your values, opinions, and feelings. These are "subjective questions." A subjective question might be:

"After a hard day's work, how do you feel?"

or

"To what extent do you think people try to take advantage of you?"

or

"How often do you feel so strongly about something that you really push and support it?"

Inexperienced interviewers may be unaware of whether their questions ask for subjective or objective information. Consequently, they frequently use sequences of questions in which they pursue a line of subjective questioning. Then, as you approach greater depth in speaking about your personal convictions, the interviewer will unknowingly break abruptly with the previous line of subjective questioning and begin asking you objective questions. Thus, the inexperienced interviewer may have lost a prime opportunity to learn more about your values, feelings, and opinions. The experienced, professional interviewer, however, will continue to ask you questions calling for subjective answers and will be able to learn a great deal about the real you. If the interviewer keeps boring in with subjective questions, you'll know you're in the hands of a pro.

Silence

There's a maxim in selling that at a certain point in the sales call, the first person who talks—salesperson or customer—loses. That is, if a salesperson can remain silent while the customer is making the buying decision, that customer is more likely to buy. If, however, the salesperson talks on past the close, he or she will lose the sale.

In the interview process, the interviewer uses silence in a similar way. There may occur a point in time in your interview when the interviewer will suddenly clam up. When this happens, you can bet that the interviewer is using this silence to embarrass you into elaborating on a sensitive subject. Or the interviewer may be testing you to see how poised you can be. Many applicants, nervous at the thought of a minute or two of silence, gush on nervously about the first thing that pops into their heads. Others sit back and try to outwait the interviewer. Either approach might show you off in the worst possible light. Let me suggest a third alternative. Give the interviewer his or her few seconds of silence. Then, after a reasonable interval has passed, politely ask: "Is there anything we haven't covered?" or "Would you like for me to elaborate on anything I've mentioned?" This puts the ball back in the interviewer's court where it belongs, and it indicates you're with the interviewer mentally, step by step.

Let's sum up

We've talked about the open-ended question, the direct question, the reflective question, and the interpretive question. We also discussed elaborating and clarifying and how they are employed, and we discussed several techniques that may be employed with you during the interview process. Remember, there is no fixed way for sequencing questions, since there are too many variables in the interviewing process. However, sometimes an interviewer may prepare and memorize a set of questions. This doesn't happen often, because it defeats the purpose of a nondirective interview. Most interviewers won't follow a set pattern. More likely, they'll jump from subject to subject.

A common approach to questioning is the use of open-ended questions early in the interview. If these produce specific information, then only encouragements and possibly clarifications will be asked of you. The interviewer will want clarification when your responses have not been very clear or when they have been too concise. While you're speaking, the interviewer will probably make mental or written notes of points that need expansion or clarification. Or the interviewer may note allusions you made to other areas that should be followed up. Any apparent contradictions made by you will be pursued. Some topics that may have been overlooked will also be noted. These may be followed up with a high proportion of direct questions and some open-ended questions in order to fill in the voids quickly.

In the course of the interview, the initiation of the topic selection will move between you and the interviewer. These shifts will be reflected by changes in question form. If the approach to questioning is mainly nondirective, you can assume you're perceived as an intelligent and articulate applicant who prefers to share in the responsibility for topic selection and development. If, on the other hand, you have difficulty in organizing your ideas and expressing yourself, you may cause the interviewer to more clearly structure the interview or to use a more directive approach. After the interview, the interviewer will interpret the data you've given. This is a crucial step in the interview process, and I talk about it in the next chapter.

5

Will the interviewer decide for or against you?

After the interview, your interviewer will go over everything he or she learned from you and will interpret it. To help the interviewer decide in your favor, you should have provided positive factors about yourself. The interviewer will have to choose between your negative and positive factors and make a judgment on what has been revealed. Keep in mind, it's never a mathematical equation. The hiring decision is always a matter of judgment. And as long as it remains this way, there are some things that should work in your favor.

Facts are not enough

Most interviewers will have little difficulty in finding out your job history, family background, health, job know-how, and so forth. However, character and personality will be judged: your mental effectiveness, your attitudes toward people, and the like. Here's where you need to be familiar with the method used by interviewers as they attempt to unravel you as a person.

Mental effectiveness and you

For one thing, you'll be judged on mental effectiveness—how effectively you use your mental abilities. If you take a test, your results will give clues to your basic ability. What does mental effectiveness mean?

- Your ability to think logically
- To express ideas precisely
- To anticipate or look ahead or plan intelligently
- To express your ideas clearly
- To get at the central issue in a problem quickly
- To spot the difference between important and unimportant matters, to display a tendency to be mentally alert, curious, and inquisitive rather than sluggish, narrow in interests, and incurious
- To possess the capacity to learn from previous experiences and to learn new material quickly

Fine, you're probably thinking, but how do I display this in an interview?

- Be precise in remembering dates, places, names.
- Be quick to grasp the meaning of questions. If you're asked a complex question such as, "What are the important things to look for in a job?," be prepared to handle it. Sort out the important from the unimportant things when you answer.
- Express your ideas with a minimum of hesitancy.

- Organize your answer to a complex question. For example, you can say, "Well, there are three things that I look for in a job: One . . . two . . . three . . ."

- Ask questions that are sharp and precise. Stay with the interviewer mentally as you talk together, and don't be passive or appear to be daydreaming.

- Be able to back up with specifics a general statement such as, "I like selling because I like people." When asked about general statements you've made, don't follow them up with even more vague generalizations. When challenged to explain a generalization ask yourself: Is it just a run-of-the-mill platitude that doesn't represent much thinking; or is it a carefully thought-through conviction that I can back up with specifics?

- Be able to explain a process, product, or situation clearly and precisely.

Your character and personality

Most interviewers will also delve into your character and personality. By character I refer to your principles and what you think is right and wrong. Personality is more a matter of whether you're interesting or dull, weak or strong, unyielding or flexible, friendly or withdrawn, mature or immature, tense or relaxed. In short, character is whether you're "good" or "bad," personality has no moral judgment in it.

- What are your values? For example, if I asked you, "Why do you want to work for my company?", how would you answer in terms of values? What's your "hot button?" Money? Challenge? Opportunity? Security?

- Are you mature and able to act your age? Indications of immaturity are self-pity, a continual use of the big "I," poor perspective on some disappointment or difficulty that has occurred in the past, excessive impulsiveness, and so on. Indications of maturity are a quiet sureness about your career goals or other personal goals; a broad perspective on the ups and downs of daily living; healthy self-honesty, a tendency to face reality, a capacity for enthusiasm without being an eager beaver, and so forth.

- How tense are you? Do you fidget or squirm, tap your fingers, swing your feet, blush easily, frown a lot, squint, or in general show outward signs of excessive inner agitation? Do you sit too still or rigid? Is your voice modulated or monotonous? What's your overall body language? (More about body language later.)

- Are you a person of convictions and quiet beliefs? Or are you highly prejudiced and emotional about what you think?

- When you talk, do you sound like a person who enjoys life? Are you enthusiastic? Interested? Alive? Is there warmth and a positive feeling to the comments you make; or are you negative or excessively detached or "dead" in feeling? Can you smile or laugh with the interviewer?

- How big is your world? Is your life bounded by job, family, physical being, or do you have outside interests? Do you belong to groups and organizations, serve in your church, participate in scouting activities, professional groups, and neighborhood gatherings? Are you genuinely concerned about the state of American business, the security of the free enterprise system?

How are your human relations?

Another key area most interviewers delve into is human relations. Here the interviewer wants to know how you relate to other people in terms of attitudes, understanding, and personal warmth.

- Do you have several close friends? Do you enjoy your family ties? Do you have a history of leadership activities such as class president, chairperson of committees, motivator in neighborhood activities?

- Do you have a sense of humor? Is it wholesome and comfortable, or do you wisecrack a lot?

- How well do you understand people? For example, when you talk about your boss, or a colleague, or a friend, can you cite specific characteristics of them? Can you analyze behavior?

- Are you self-assertive? If the interviewer objects to something you've said, can you good-humoredly stick to your guns? Do you argue or differ tactfully? Do you ask penetrating questions? For example, if you asked me to tell you two or three basic things about my company, would you make me perform nicely for you?

How do you view yourself?

Interviewers will often focus their attention on how much insight you possess about yourself. Such insight is the capacity to see into yourself, to look behind your obvious and overt behavior. Insight, particularly self-insight, is a most difficult capacity to analyze. The following story illustrates what I mean.

A man and three companions are dining in a public restaurant. The man is so involved in relating an experience he's just been through that gradually he talks louder and longer. His companions are politely interested at first; then they begin to glance at one another and at nearby tables to see how others are reacting to the loud talking. They diddle with their food; and although they all want to shush the man, no one does. Suddenly, he realizes how long and loud he's been talking. He gains insight and sees

himself as others see him. He lowers his voice and con-
cludes his story.

For your interviewer to get an idea of your insight into
yourself, your capacity to see yourself "as others see you,"
he or she will ask questions that will give clues as to how
you see yourself in relation to others. Your interviewer can
do this by asking you to describe your best friend, then
following that up with a question asking you to describe
the differences between you and your best friend. You
could also be asked to define such terms as *leadership*, or
integrity, or *success*, and even *insight*.

One of the worst answers I get when I ask candidates
to tell me about their weaknesses (preceded by a question
asking about their strengths), is; "I don't have any weaknesses." Any interviewer with any experience or common
sense would view that response as totally lacking in the
ability to see the self as others see you. Don't let yourself
fall into that category. Convince the interviewer you can
look at yourself as others do and that you have insight into
your weaknesses as well as your strengths.

Are you supervisory material?

If you're applying for a supervisory position, you may
be examined in terms of your ability to make judgments
concerning others. Obviously, the other areas we
discussed—mental effectiveness, character and personality, relations with others, and insight—count toward
supervisory ability. Then, too, the interviewer may look
for special characteristics in you.

• Are you a "take-charge" person?

- Are you someone who plans your life carefully to reach specific goals?
- Are you capable of motivating others to put forth their best efforts?
- Do you have a contagious enthusiasm?
- Can you make decisions without having all the facts?
- Are you a natural leader?
- Can you seek out a consensus of opinion and test out your decision in your mind?

In other words, supervisory ability is your total impact if you were in charge of a group—how you would affect that group, influence it, and lead it to provide results that would enable you to accomplish your goals. Here's how to project the image of supervisory ability:

- In school and previous work situations at one time or another, you might have been chairperson, president, or leader. If you were "on top" of the situation in those jobs, don't hesitate to let the interviewer know it.
- If given a chance in an interview, move in and take charge. Ask questions. Direct the course of the conversation and assume responsibility for the end result.
- As you talk about your "best" or "worst" boss, show that you have a feeling for the boss's responsibilities. Let your criticisms be indicative of an accurate perception on your part about the job of the supervisor.
- The interviewer suddenly disagrees with you, but don't fold up. Instead, tactfully state your position without being overly solicitous, or rigid, or insistent on your point of view.
- Show how you use your spare time in a way that indicates a "take-charge" kind of person. Think of projects you've

completed or neighborhood activities you've organized; maybe you've run a social or headed up a condominium committee. Don't keep it a secret.

Other characteristics liable to be assessed will depend a great deal on the level of the position you're applying for. You may be evaluated on your accomplishments in meeting objectives such as profit and revenue targets or cost objectives. The interviewer may pass judgment on you relative to your ability to:

- Produce work in a high volume without sacrificing quality or cutting corners
- Deal with community or government representatives in a sensitive and productive manner
- Manage your segment of a business with respect to equal employment opportunity in both the spirit and letter of the law;
- Show appropriate concern in taking action where safety is required and to meet legal requirements
- Perform so as to ensure good customer relations and exhibit sensitivity to unusual problems
- Practice and recognize the need for sound employee recruitment
- Instill high levels of motivation and commitment among subordinates
- Help subordinates grow and develop
- Provide leadership
- Consider all available information before making an important decision
- Display sensitivity to the "people" element, where decisions require coordination and teamwork

- Respond to feedback and change your course when it becomes clear that a plan of action is not working as intended
- Have knowledge of your field by being acquainted with current ideas, techniques, trends, discoveries, and the state of the art
- Weigh complex information and arrive at sound conclusions
- Be counted on to carry out assignments thoroughly, promptly, and accurately
- Willingly take risks for the sake of improving the organization
- Display drive and ambition by willingly taking the initiative, persistently seeking goals, and exerting extra effort to succeed
- Display self-confidence without being arrogant
- Convince others by presenting one's point of view logically
- Stand up to stress in the face of unusual pressure
- Be aware and sensitive to the needs, fears, feelings of others and to be able to work productively with individuals and with groups of diverse personalities

We could keep adding to this list. But I hope I've given you some idea of the criteria used in judging a supervisory candidate.

The interviewer will also be assessing the overall impact you make as a candidate. Did you inspire the interviewer or leave him or her cold? Were you interesting or dull? Did you display personal warmth and charm? Did you show energy and enthusiasm? Or did you act as if you were dead from the ankles up? In short, did you attract or repel the interviewer?

Now let me give you one final list before we close this chapter. How well do you score on the following points?

- Neatness
- Poise
- Tact
- Courtesy (Don't assume you're on a first-name basis with the interviewer.)
- Confidence
- Warmth
- Enthusiasm
- Cheerfulness
- Optimism
- Humor
- A firm handshake
- Good pronunciation
- Good vocabulary
- Good grammar
- A clear, organized manner of expression

Beginning with that firm, initial handshake, the interviewer should sense that you're exceptional. Now, let me lead you through a typical interview to demonstrate how everything comes together.

6

Dissecting the interview

Admittedly, you can't rehearse your interview role. You don't know who the interviewer will be or where the interviewer will lead you. You can, however, prepare yourself for almost any kind of interview if you can recognize certain techniques and if you understand how the interviewer is gathering information about you. I've reproduced a typical interview to give you an opportunity (1) to gain an understanding of the thought process that provides the background for the interviewer's actions; and (2) to provide you with a sample of what you can expect during an interview.

There are three parts to the dialogue. First, there is what the interviewer actually says; second, what the interviewer is thinking; and third, how the interviewee responds. As you read the dialogue and "listen in" on the interviewer's thoughts, you'll better understand what goes on in the interviewer's mind as he or she tries to unravel the background, experience, and personal characteristics of you, the candidate.

Mary Gorham is interviewing a candidate named Bob Jones. Bob is looking for a job as a salesman. The third "voice" in the dialogue is Mary Gorham's thoughts. As you read the dialogue, try to identify with Mary. By putting yourself in her shoes, you'll gain better insight and understanding into the interviewer's objectives and stratagems. This understanding will increase your ability to deal with that real-life interviewer.

The interview begins

Scene

The interview is about to take place. The person conducting the interview is Mrs. Mary Gorham. She is the personnel manager for the International Apex Company. As a result of earlier interviews, she has screened out all but four candidates for a sales job. Bob Jones is one of the four candidates who remain in the running. Whether or not he gets the job will depend to a great extent on how well this interview goes. Here, now, is the interview.

MRS. GORHAM'S

ALTER EGO: *As a result of the screening process, I have identified a number of candidates I think can do this job. Today, I plan to conduct interviews with four of those candidates. I will spend approximately one-half hour with each candidate; and hopefully, I will be able to make a determination as to whether or not I have any interest in them for future employment.*

The first candidate is a fellow by the name of Robert M.

Jones. I have read Mr. Jones' résumé and application, and he is presently waiting in the lobby. I will now go out and greet him.

MRS. GORHAM: Good day, Mr. Jones. I am Mary Gorham, the personnel manager.

MR. JONES: Hi, I'm Bob Jones. Pleased to meet you.

ALTER EGO: *In order to establish some rapport, I'll ask him about his trip over here. I will do it in a manner that makes it very easy for him to respond.*

MRS. GORHAM: Did you have any trouble finding us with the directions we gave you?

MR. JONES: Oh, no. Your instructions were very clear. No problems whatsoever.

ALTER EGO: *I'll lead him back into the office now; and to make it less awkward, I will tell him that I will lead the way.*

MRS. GORHAM: Bob, let's go to my office where we can chat. I'll lead the way, OK?

MR. JONES: Fine.

ALTER EGO: *I prefer to interview candidates using two chairs not quite facing each other, as opposed to other arrangements, such as from behind a desk. I feel that interviewing over a desk creates a barrier to good two-way communication.*

MRS. GORHAM: Have a seat, Bob. Make yourself comfortable. Would you like a cup of coffee?

MR. JONES: I would, very much.

ALTER EGO: *I will help make him more comfortable by treating him with the consideration due a guest.*

MRS. GORHAM: How would you like your coffee, Bob?

MR. JONES: Oh, regular. Just one sugar and some milk.

ALTER EGO: *He can sit here and get used to the office and relax a little while I go down and get the coffee.*

MRS. GORHAM: Fine, I'll be right back.

MR. JONES: OK, thanks.

MRS. GORHAM: Hi, I'm back. Here you are.

MR. JONES: Thank you.

ALTER EGO: *Now, on with the interview.*

MRS. GORHAM: Bob, as I mentioned earlier, I am Mary Gorham, the personnel manager for International Apex.

ALTER EGO: *That's it; tell him specifically who you are and why you are here.*

MRS. GORHAM: We are looking for a salesperson.

ALTER EGO: *That's it. Mention to him at this point that you'll be taking notes, so that he will not be alarmed or concerned as you write.*

MRS. GORHAM: As I talk to you this morning, I will be making notes on both your résumé and your application.

MR. JONES: Fine.

The interviewer decides on a point in time in the applicant's past whereupon to start her data gathering.

ALTER EGO: *In looking over the paper work, I notice that this applicant has been out of school for a long time; therefore, I don't feel it necessary to start back in college. However, I may want to come back to that later. I think with this applicant, the best place to start would probably be with the first job after college. I'll ask an open-ended question about that job. I'll preface it with a few remarks, so that we can lead into the interview in a comfortable fashion.*

The interviewer formulates a hypothesis about the candidate. She will check out this hypothesis throughout the interview by asking questions from time to time that will either prove or disprove her hypothesis.

ALTER EGO: *I also notice that he was a manager at one time; hence I will form a hypothesis that says that this candidate is more in-*

terested in a management position and that he is only applying for this position with the thought in mind of using it as a steppingstone out of direct sales and into management.

MRS. GORHAM: As a starting point, I would like to go back to your first job after college. Can you tell me a little bit about that job?

MR. JONES: Certainly. After graduating from Boston College, where I majored in economics, I was looking for a position that would utilize my educational background. At that time, the Peerless Company was conducting interviews on campus, and I had interviewed with the campus recruiter. I think during that period of time, I must have interviewed with maybe four or five various companies; however, the Peerless position seemed to be very much in line with my objectives. I had been very interested in marketing, and the Peerless position offered an opportunity for me to start in sales and, hopefully, to learn the marketing field from the ground up.

The interviewer needs to gather data that is relevant to the job description.

ALTER EGO: *I need some more information about what the job at Peerless consisted of, so that I can judge if that experience is relevant to the criteria for our opening. Specifically, I need to know if the work required a high energy level, working with high-level contacts, selling skills, perseverance, activity, interaction with customers and superiors, and report requirements; and what his overall job, responsibilities, and achievements were. To get at this, I'll ask him an open-ended question.*

MRS. GORHAM: Would you tell me about your position at Peerless . . . what it involved on a day–to–day basis?

MR. JONES: Yes, I'd be glad to. I started with Peerless in July, shortly after I graduated from college. I was placed in a

training program, where I learned how to be a retail salesman for the packaged soap group. This position was in the
northeast district. I won several district and many unit
awards for sales performance; and as a result of that, I was
promoted and moved up to the position of district head
salesman, roughly around October of the following year.
After having succeeded in that position, I was then promoted to the district head salesman for the New Jersey
area, and I had to relocate there. I worked on special assignments in New Jersey under the guidance of the district
manager, and I was completely responsible for one major
chain. In addition, I successfully sold the fourth size of one
product that was never carried before in that chain.

The interviewer did not understand a point, so she will ask
for clarification of it.

ALTER EGO: *The fourth size of a product—what does that mean? I'm
not sure I understand. I'll ask him a direct question.*

MRS. GORHAM: What is the fourth size of a product?

MR. JONES: That's where we had a giant economy size, a large
size, a regular size, and a fourth size that was called the
family-size package. It fell between the giant economy size
and the regular. These sizes, of course, were created by our
marketing staff to meet consumer needs.

MRS. GORHAM: I see. Go on.

MR. JONES: In May I was promoted to unit manager, and I had
responsibility for Unit C out of Columbus, Ohio, which had
a sales volume of over six million dollars. At that point in
time, I had six salesmen reporting to me. The unit territory
covered a small portion of Ohio, two counties in Kentucky,
and about half the state of West Virginia.

MRS. GORHAM: What else did you achieve as unit manager?

MR. JONES: Well, at that time, the unit had two vacancies and was seventeenth out of twenty-two units in the central division. By December of that year, we had moved to the fifth position, and all sections were filled by me; and a new brand was introduced into the area. At that time, all of our major accounts were buying three sizes of the products.

ALTER EGO: *It sounds like he was very successful with Peerless. I wonder why he left. I'll ask a direct question and find out.*

MRS. GORHAM: I see that you left the firm shortly thereafter, in March. Why was that?

MR. JONES: Basically, I left because of money; I was only earning around eleven thousand dollars a year. At that time, an opportunity came up for me to start my own firm, and I did so.

ALTER EGO: *It appears to me that this employee left for a good reason; so I will now go into his second job, as president of his own firm. I'll ask an open-ended question.*

MRS. GORHAM: I see from your application that you were president of a firm called The American Distributors, Incorporated, in Greenville. Could you tell me about that firm?

MR. JONES: Yes, as I was saying, I left Peerless to start my own firm. It was organized by me with approximately one thousand dollars capitalization, and the object of the firm was to merchandize women's hosiery products in drug and grocery outlets. I handled all phases of the operation. As we were fairly successful, I added two people for servicing and inventory.

ALTER EGO: *This fellow seems to be entrepreneurial in spirit, and I wonder how well the firm did over the years and whether or not he was successful. I will ask him a direct question in that regard.*

MRS. GORHAM: Would you tell me about your business; was it profitable?

MR. JONES: Well, yes and no. Sales volume was approximately $69,000; and then it grew over a three-year period to ap-

proximately $150,000; and then it slid back to approxi-
mately $36,000. I actually lost money.

ALTER EGO: *I wonder why it slid back. I'll ask an open-ended question and let him elaborate.*

MRS. GORHAM: Why was that?

The candidate wants to demonstrate his mental effectiveness, so he will answer the question precisely.

MR. JONES: Well, it was a combination of three things. First, we
were undercapitalized. Second of all, hosiery prices became
depressed at all levels by 50 to 100 percent; and third, the
general economic conditions at those times capsized the
venture.

ALTER EGO: *I like the way he answered that question. Specifically, I like the way he answered, giving three reasons . . . one, two, three. It shows that he has good mental effectiveness. I don't, however, like the fact that the business failed. I need to know more.*

MRS. GORHAM: What happened then?

MR. JONES: Well, in July I sold all the accounts to a larger dis-
tributor; and I might add that I got out of the business at
just about the right time, because the conditions that I
mentioned earlier got even worse before they got better.

ALTER EGO: *The next job that he had was with Century Corporation. I'm going to lead into that now and find out what that job involved. I'll do that with an open-ended question, with a little introduction for some transfer.*

MRS. GORHAM: I see that in August of that year, after disposing
of your business, you joined the Century Corporation. Can
you tell me about that position?

MR. JONES: Yes, I'd be glad to. I don't know if you saw the ads
that Century was running at the time; however, they were
touting the business as being a future-growth star. They

were offering equity positions. I felt that my background and experience, plus the types of things that I like doing—pretty much being on my own—all pointed toward exploring further the possibilities of joining a firm such as Century Corporation. I contacted them and interviewed with them. This resulted in their hiring me as a regional representative.

ALTER EGO: *Regional representative sounds to me like a direct sales job. I will ask an open-ended question and find out exactly what this job involved.*

MRS. GORHAM: What did your job as a regional representative involve?

MR. JONES: I was directly responsible for handling franchise dealers. This involved answering inquiries and making sales calls on people with audio-visual authority in libraries, schools, and businesses.

ALTER EGO: *In other words, he was actually making direct sales calls on potential customers. I need to know more. I'll ask him to elaborate and clarify.*

MRS. GORHAM: Tell me more about your interaction with franchise dealers.

MR. JONES: Century had set up a number of franchise dealers in the New England states. They were independent businessmen who marketed audio-visual products directly to libraries, schools, and businesses within specific geographic territories. My job involved working with these franchise dealers and assisting them in making sales calls, so they could get their businesses up and running. Century Corporation, the parent, received a percentage of the revenue from each franchise dealer; hence it was in their best interest for the franchise dealers to do well.

ALTER EGO: *Well, I could have him elaborate and clarify even further, but I think I have a pretty good idea as to what his job consisted of. It was primarily interfacing with the franchise dealers and helping them close business. I think I have a good idea of what he was doing. Therefore, I'll ask him an open-ended question as to why he left Century.*

MRS. GORHAM: Can you tell me why you left Century?

MR. JONES: Yes, very simply, the firm ran into severe financial difficulty; and as a result, the majority of the staff was placed on reduction-in-force.

ALTER EGO: *Generally when companies place people on reduction-in-force, if there are no seniority considerations, they furlough the least productive members of the team. Could it be that this individual falls into that category? I will ask him some more questions so that he can elaborate and clarify the situation for me.*

MRS. GORHAM: About how many people did Century Corporation let go at that time?

MR. JONES: Oh, I would say in the neighborhood of fifteen people.

MRS. GORHAM: Out of how many?

MR. JONES: Oh, roughly out of twenty people on staff.

MRS. GORHAM: Well, why weren't you one of the five people they retained?

MR. JONES: I'm not quite sure what criteria they used to retain the five people and let the other fifteen go; however, I will say that had they offered me the opportunity to stay with the firm, I probably would not have done so.

ALTER EGO: *Well, let's see here now. This sounds a little bit unusual. There must be more to the situation than meets the eye. Maybe I had better ask an open-ended question and see where it goes from there.*

MRS. GORHAM.:   Can you explain in a little more detail what you mean?

MR. JONES: Yes, basically the situation at Century was that the franchisees were running into a great deal of difficulty in marketing the AV product, because technically, the materials were not compatible with the equipment that was generally found in most AV departments in the libraries, schools, and businesses. As a result of this, the sales were not where they should have been. Correspondingly, the revenues were way down. A lot of people that had invested in the business were fearful that they would lose their entire investments. That time, Century announced they were cutting back on staff. The severance arrangements were such that I felt it was a good time to more or less pick up my marbles and leave the game. Had they offered me the opportunity to stay on, I seriously doubt that I would have, as the business looked to me like it was going to get progressively worse. At the time that I left Century, I was given fairly decent outplacement assistance and, I might add, enough salary continuance to tide me over until I could find another job.

The candidate assesses his answer at this point and decides that a more specific answer is in order. If he is to dispel any doubts the interviewer might have as to why he was let go, he must do so now.

MR. JONES (CONTINUED):   To answer your question more specifically as to why they picked five and let the rest of us go, all I can say is that I really do not know, other than the fact that they probably had their own reasons. I do not feel the five people they retained were any better qualified or more productive than the fifteen that were let go, and I certainly can assure you that my record with Century was as good, if not better, than those of the individuals they offered to retain.

ALTER EGO: *Well, that was a pretty good response. I'll let him reflect on that a little and see where he goes with it.*

MRS. GORHAM: Then you feel that you did a pretty good job at Century and should have been retained?

MR. JONES: Yes, that's correct. I feel that during the short time I was with them, I did a thorough job in covering my assigned responsibilities, and any problems that developed were not my doing. Rather, the base cause of them was the failure of the products to be compatible with existing audio-visual equipment that was out there in the market place.

ALTER EGO: *So much for his work history. I think what I'd like to do now is get into his personality. I'll ask an open-ended question.*

MRS. GORHAM: Would you tell me about what you believe to be your strong points as a person?

The interviewee, Bob Jones, has anticipated this line of questioning and can now furnish good, solid answers.

MR. JONES: Well, let me think about that one a minute. I think that basically my strongest point is my ability to get along with people, both my peers, my superiors, and my subordinates. I have always excelled in what you might call interpersonal relations.

MRS. GORHAM: I'd be interested in knowing what you believe to be some of your weak points as a person.

MR. JONES: Everyone has some weaknesses and I've got my weak points. If I were to single one out, I would probably say that it was my inability to relax away from the job. I always seem to be concerned about what's going on in my territory or what's happening back at the office, and I frequently take a lot of work home with me. I have a hard time unwinding from the job and relaxing.

ALTER EGO: *Well, that was a pretty good response. In fact, he used that question to his advantage and answered it by responding in a manner that shows me his weakness is really a strength when it comes to working. That was good. Now, I think I'll ask him about what some of the qualities are that he admires in other people. This will give me some insight into his personality and also into how he views himself.*

MRS. GORHAM: Would you tell me about the qualities that you admire in other people?

Here, again, the candidate has anticipated this line of questioning and can provide a good answer.

MR. JONES: Yes, I think that I can answer that question. I think that the prime qualities I admire in other people are honesty and integrity and above all, people that are real human beings.

ALTER EGO: *Well, I could use some elaborating and clarifying on that last portion, so I'll have him elaborate a little further by asking an open-ended question.*

MRS. GORHAM: Perhaps you can clarify what you mean by "real human beings."

MR. JONES: Yes, I think that one of the qualities I admire most in people is when they come across as being "real human beings." I mean all people have strengths and weaknesses, but some pretend to be "supermen" or "superwomen." Very often, in my business career, I have encountered people who put up a great big facade and try to play the role; however, it has been my experience that these people always get caught-up-with in the end and are losers. On the other hand, I have worked for and with people who were genuine human beings, and this came through in their everyday interactions with others. They did not pretend to be anything other than what they were, nor did they promise anything that they could not deliver. I can honestly say that I'd take a genuine human being over the other kind any day.

The interviewer wants to hear some more about this. She may be onto a negative aspect of the candidate. She will probe deeper.

ALTER EGO: *Let's get into this a little deeper. Ask some more questions, and we'll get some better insight into his character and personality.*

MRS. GORHAM: Can you tell me about what irritates you or displeases you most in other people?

MR. JONES: Well, I think we were just talking about that to some degree. I think one of the things that irritates or displeases me most in other people is when they pretend to be something that they are not. The type of individual who on one occasion slaps you on the back and on another occasion stabs you in the back. I would much prefer an individual who is open and honest to one who is closed and deceitful.

ALTER EGO: *This could be a clue to his personality. I wonder if he ever really gets angry at people. I'll ask him what makes him angry.*

MRS. GORHAM: I'd be interested in knowing about the last incident that made you angry.

MR. JONES: Gee, that's a tough question. I really don't recall when I've been angry the last time.

ALTER EGO: *Well, he's surely been angry at some time in his life. Maybe I'll bounce it off him again by using a reflective question.*

MRS. GORHAM: You mean you haven't been angry in a long time?

MR. JONES: Well, yes, I guess you can say that; but looking back, I think that probably the last time I got angry is when this woman left her empty shopping cart in the parking lot of the supermarket, and the wind caught it; it rolled into the side of my car, and it not only scratched it but put a dent in it.

ALTER EGO: *I'd have to agree with him, that would irritate me a little, too; but I still have to find out more about his personality, so I'll ask him another open-ended question.*

MRS. GORHAM: Would you explain what you did about it?

MR. JONES: Well, there wasn't much that I could do about it. After all, the woman didn't push the cart into my car intentionally. It was more or less an act of God—the wind caught it, and it just sailed along until it banged into the car. About all I could do was get out of the car and look over toward where the woman was and sort of give her a dirty look. I then set the cart up so it wouldn't move anymore.

The candidate pulled that one out of the fire and may have even enhanced his position.

ALTER EGO: *Well, that was a good answer. It indicates to me that this candidate is grown up and is mature. It also indicates to me that the individual has a broad perspective on the ups and downs of daily living and a tendency to look at reality squarely.*

The interviewer has been satisfied up to this point. She now seeks more relevant information and considers new areas to delve into, new places to follow her hypotheses and check them out.

ALTER EGO: *I could go on and pursue character and personality to find out more about the candidate's values. I could go into the subject of money, challenge, opportunity, security . . . I can find out if the candidate is a person of convictions and quiet beliefs or if he is highly prejudiced and emotional about what he thinks. I can also get some indications on this candidate's personality by just listening to the noises he makes. He appears to be making noises like a person who enjoys life and is enthusiastic, interested, and alive. There is also a good warmth and positiveness of feeling to the comments that he is making. I think that I have a pretty good idea of where this candidate stands in terms of his personality. I think the next area that I would like to explore is his ambitions. At the same time that I explore the ambitions, I would like to loop back to my earlier question about whether or not this individual wants to stay in sales or whether he wants a management role. I will also check out the hypothesis that I have formed earlier about this candidate's wanting to be a manager rather than a salesperson. I will get at all three of these with an open-ended question.*

MRS. GORHAM: I'd be interested in knowing what position you want to hold several years from now.

MR. JONES: Well, as you know, I am interested in a direct selling position in the short term, because I feel that this is where my real strengths lie. I also feel that a direct salesperson can earn substantially more money than a person in a management position can. Hence, at this point in time and for the next several years, I see myself in the role of a direct salesperson working on some sort of incentive program where I can earn substantial amounts of money.

ALTER EGO: *Well, what he's telling me is that he wants to stay in direct sales for a number of years, but he still has not answered my question to my satisfaction; so I will ask him to elaborate and clarify a little. I will use a direct question for this.*

MRS. GORHAM: In a few years from now, then, do you still see yourself as a direct salesperson?

MR. JONES: Yes, I see myself three years from now in an established territory with established accounts, performing the role of a direct salesperson. I do not see myself as a manager at the present time. Maybe after five years or so, I would be ready to step into a manager's position, but not until I have proven to my own satisfaction that I am an outstanding salesperson whose earnings are only limited by his own abilities.

ALTER EGO: *I'm still not sure that I understand where he wants to be several years from now. Maybe I'd better ask him another open-ended question and check out my hypothesis even further.*

MRS. GORHAM: I'm not certain I understand where you plan to be several years from now. Could you explain in a little more detail?

MR. JONES: Yes, in a few years from now I plan to be in a direct selling position. I want my earnings to reflect my ability, and I believe that the only way this can be achieved in the short term—and by that I mean three to five years—is by having my salary and commissions tied directly to my performance. The only way that I'm aware that this can be done, in your organization, is in a direct selling position.

ALTER EGO: *OK, that was a pretty conclusive answer. I think I'll ask one more question about ambitions and then I'll move along. I think I'll ask him a question that will give me some insight into his own self-image.*

MRS. GORHAM: Can you tell me about the reputation you like to enjoy as an employee?

MR. JONES: Gee, you ask some good questions, but I can answer that. The reputation that I like to enjoy as an employee is that of being an honest person, a genuine human being, and a person who deals fair and square with other people in all walks of life. I consider myself to be a solid member of the community, and I feel that I am a good, solid individual who performs a useful role in society. I also consider myself to be a self-starter and a hard worker. I believe in the work ethic, and I enjoy being perceived as a contributor to bottom-line results.

ALTER EGO: *Well, that was a good answer. At this point in time, I can carry on this interview along the same lines, asking reflective questions and interpretive questions, open-ended questions and direct questions, and getting into more elaborating and clarifying questions. I could also form some more hypotheses, and I can look to comments that were made earlier in the interview. I would just like to take a few moments to review this interview thus far. First of all,*

I'd like to reflect on this employee's appearance. How does this candidate impress me? Does this candidate create a better-than-average appearance? An excellent appearance? Or somewhat less than an ordinary appearance? Does this candidate inspire me, or does he leave me cold? Is the candidate interesting or dull? Does he have personal warmth and charm, or does he repel me? Does this candidate appear neat and robust, with good posture, good facial expression? Is he tactful, courteous, confident, warm, enthusiastic, cheerful, optimistic, animated, and humorous? Does the applicant have good pronunciation, vocabulary, grammar? Does the applicant express himself freely, with clarity, in an organized manner? And has the applicant exhibited good mental effectiveness, good character and personality, and good skill in human relations? Does this applicant have insight?

In short, looking over this candidate up to this point, from the beginning of the interview until now, have I sensed that he is exceptional and likely to be hired? Well, I think I do, so at this point in time I will continue to interview him and get back into his individual work pattern and some of the more specific requirements of this particular position. Before I do that, I will give him the opportunity to open up new areas by allowing him to ask me questions.

MRS. GORHAM: Well, Mr. Jones, thank you very much for your time. Do you have any questions that you would like to ask me?

At this point the interviewee, Bob Jones, can ask questions; the better the questions, the better he will be evaluated. These questions should be thought through beforehand. The interviewer will continue to evaluate and judge, ask questions and formulate hypotheses, and so forth; so do not assume for one moment that you are in control. Make every question and every answer count . . . and you will win!

7

Don't let your body language give you away

It's not always what you say;
It's how you say it

Is it possible to communicate with another person without using words? You bet it is. Nonverbals can carry many times the weight of verbals. Nonverbals, or body language, involve body movement such as of the head and limbs. It also has to do with the way we position ourselves in relation to one another, how we time our verbal exchanges, the amount of eye–to–eye contact, and the where, how, and how often we touch each other. In the interview situation, you're engaged in a face–to–face conversation. Normally, you'll become so involved in what's being said that you may not realize you're sending out clues that may give an additional meaning to the message you're trying to convey to the interviewer. What you do with your body and how you move provides many clues to the interviewer. It tells how you feel about yourself and others. The casual movement of your shoulders or the posture you assume can provide infinitely more signals than the actual words you utter.

Let's say you're halfway through an interview that, if successful, can result in a job offer. Suddenly you get a sinking feeling. Something is wrong. By the time the interview is over, you have a gut feeling that tells you you've blown it. But how? You answered all the questions superbly; you were up for the interview, and you gave it your best shot. You felt you were doing fine; then all of a sudden—almost imperceptibly,—the interviewer sat back, crossed his arms over his chest, and started to fire direct questions at you, one after another. Up to that point, he had asked mainly open-ended questions and had given you ample time to answer each one. Now it appeared that he was anxious to get the interview over with, and he was speeding it along. Sure enough, several days later you get a write-off letter telling you that you were rejected. But you knew as soon as you left the interview that you had blown it. How? By the silent, nonverbal body language that the interviewer sent out when you were selling yourself.

The importance of nonverbal communication can't be emphasized enough. In the face–to–face interview situation, your message is being communicated by more than just words, and it is being received by more than a passive body with only ears acting as receptacles of information. The listening body also has eyes. By using the language of your body to make your verbal communication more effective, you'll bring about an increased understanding of your abilities. Further, if you're sensitive to the signs the interviewer is giving off, you'll be better able to determine how well or how poorly you're doing and adjust your behavior accordingly.

Most of us view oral communication as an exchange of words and ideas. We tend to overlook the role that attitudes and emotions play in communications. Facial expressions, movement of limbs, slight gestures, often reveal more than the spoken word does. It's interesting to note that nonverbal clues can contradict a spoken message. A silly example of this can be demonstrated by moving your head up and down and saying "no" or by moving your head from side to side and saying "yes."

If, on the other hand, the nonverbal supports the verbal, then the verbal message is vastly more persuasive. For example, when you move your head up and down and say "yes," you're strengthening your message. If you increase the up-and-down movement, you'll indicate an increased amount of agreement or acceptance; and your "yes" takes on a greater degree of meaning. Now you're conveying the message that you really do agree with what you're hearing. The accompanying nonverbal supported your statement and made it much more persuasive. So it is with all nonverbals: They can alter, modify, enhance, detract, negate, reinforce, or contradict the meaning of the spoken word. Because the interview consists primarily of a verbal exchange, it's important for you to be aware of the impact nonverbals can have on the dialogue.

An inexact science, but . . .

Psychologists have conducted studies on the way that body language modifies the meaning of the spoken word. On one side of the coin, they know that no body position or movement in and of itself has a precise meaning. The infinite variety of movement of parts of the body—such as the head, arms, and legs—the way we position ourselves in relation to others, the timing of verbal exchanges, the amount and kinds of eye contact, and how often people touch one another do not give full meaning all by themselves. Only when the spoken language and the body language are used together do we get the full meaning of what a person is saying.

By being aware of body language, you can use it to your advantage in the interview situation. As you receive and interpret signals others are sending out, you can monitor your own signals. You can achieve greater control over yourself, and in turn, you will function more effectively.

A word of caution, however. It's difficult to do; if you try on a conscious level to project a certain message, you run the risk of doing it wrong or of mishandling it. Sometimes, if you become self-conscious about what you are doing, it becomes more difficult to do. Here, then, is what I recommend: Play it safe. We are going to focus our attention on the body language of the interviewer, so that we can monitor his or her messages. During the interview, you should be aware of your own body language; but you should not consciously try to modify it to any great extent unless you feel confident in doing so. The interview situation is not the place to practice. Too much is at stake!

As you observe the interviewer, you should be looking for movements or gestures that will give you clues to his or her thinking. For example, if the interviewer suddenly sits back and folds his or her arms abruptly, you can be pretty sure that trouble has arrived. A suppressed smile, a lifted eyebrow, or a wrinkling of the nose can tell you how the interviewer is reacting to what you are saying. Those messages, if properly interpreted, can provide you with steady feedback as you talk. As the interviewer listens to what you're saying, you should look for signs of reception or rejection. For example, if the interviewer's eyes are looking down, covered by his or her eyelids, or if the face is turned away, or if the smile does not involve the cheeks or the nostrils (i.e., the creases around the eyes are not deepened), then you're being shut out. The interviewer has turned off and tuned you out. If, however, the interviewer's mouth is relaxed and void of any smile, with the chin forward and eyes gazing sideways but not directly at you, then he or she is partially with you and is considering what you're saying.

If the interviewer's eyes engage yours and hold them for several seconds at a time with a slight smile extending at least to the cheeks, then he or she is with you and is evaluating what you're saying. Finally, if the interviewer shifts his or her head and faces you squarely with an expansive smile engaging the cheeks, the nostrils, and the creases around the eyes, along with good eye contact, then he or she is enthusiastic about you. The interviewer is open and receptive to everything you have to say.

Your body doesn't know how to lie

It's a fact—your body does not know how to lie. Every movement you make gives off a message, and that message emphasizes or contradicts your verbals. If you're timid or fearful during the interview, you may show it by holding a tense posture, by hunching your shoulders, pulling in your chin, or holding your eyes open wide. If you're confident, it will show. You will lean forward slightly, indicating a relaxed, highly interested participant. If you're arrogant or overconfident, you might assume a backward sprawl, which might even signal disrespect for the interviewer. If you're depressed or suffering from defeat by not being able to land a job, you might signal that defeat by holding your head forward, sunken, and resting on your chest, with eyes downcast. If you're a good persuader, you probably will use slow, easy gestures; a resonant, inflective voice, with a ring of optimism; an uplifted chin; composed hands; you will keep your head on an even plane with the interviewer and maintain good face–to–face eye contact and slow, regular breathing.

Whatever your mood is, and whatever level of confidence you possess, it will show through during the interview. If your mood is negative or if your level of confidence is low, you must make an effort not to broadcast it with your body language. Your body language has to depict a high level of confidence. It should enhance and reinforce your verbals, so that you come across to the interviewer in the most positive light, and therefore in the most advantageous manner.

A word of caution

By now you realize that there's no precise formula for interpreting the various aspects of body language. No hard and fast rules exist. Interpreting the language of the body is more intuitive than anything else. You can, however, sharpen your intuition and awareness of body language by observing the interactions of others at work, in restaurants, and in social situations. Make mental notes of the body language they use to modify the spoken word, and internalize them.

When you play the game for keeps in front of that job interviewer, your body language must reinforce the truth behind the words. You also must observe the body language of the interviewer for signs of acceptance or rejection of your message, then adjust your delivery accordingly. I don't expect you to change overnight the body language you have developed in a lifetime. I do, however, expect you'll increase your awareness of the importance that body language plays in communication. That awareness will enhance your ability to win in your job interview ... that and preparation for in-depth questions. You'll learn about this aspect in the next chapter.

8

Questions you can expect

During the interview you will be asked specific questions. These questions will cover many aspects of your background and experience, your values and feelings, and your aspirations and objectives. As you know by now, the interviewer will be using open-ended questions to get you to reveal as much about yourself as possible. The more you elaborate, the more you'll reveal. The more you reveal, the more data the interviewer will have with which to judge you as a candidate. The interviewer will pursue the subject matter in depth and will be able to do so in a very effective manner.

By asking how, why, what, when, and where, all aspects of any subject can be systematically explored. To prepare for this type of in-depth questioning, you must look past the first question and be prepared for the second, third, and fourth. If the interviewer has asked for the how, you can be sure the why, what, when and where of it will follow.

You must also be able to answer all questions in a manner that indicates you have good mental effectiveness. (Remember? We discussed mental effectiveness earlier.) You should have thought through your answers carefully, so they present you in the best possible light. This means you must play up your good points. You certainly don't want to reveal your bad points.

I've compiled questions that are most likely to come up during your interview and have broken them down into nine categories. These are: early childhood environment, education, job history, feelings about past jobs, feelings toward people, job objectives, your self-image, conditions of work, and miscellaneous. Within each category, I've itemized a set of questions that includes the initial question—generally an open-ended question—followed up by an in-depth probe consisting of how, why, what, when, or where. For each category I've also included the reasons behind the question. If you understand what the interviewer is after, you'll be better able to provide a positive answer. Once again, as you read the questions, formulate your own responses by carefully thinking through your own personal circumstances. Your answers should be ones you're comfortable with and ones that will prove beneficial to you and work toward your being selected for the job.

Early childhood environment

Your early home life and upbringing can provide valuable clues to an interviewer about your character, interests, motivation, values, personality, and sense of responsibleness. Because this aspect of your life is personal, it's extremely difficult for an interviewer to get into; he or she must handle it with skill and sensitivity.

To further compound this subject, a number of areas are taboo, according to the Office of Equal Employment Opportunity. However, if the interviewer does get into this area, you should be prepared (see Chapter 10). Your answers must be thought out beforehand. Make sure your reactions and responses don't work against you by diminishing the rapport built up between you and the interviewer. If you're prepared beforehand, you should be able to handle any question with a solid response. Here are the questions:

> "Tell me about your home life while you were growing up."
>
> "What line of work was your father in?"
>
> "What was your father like?"
>
> "How many brothers and sisters do you have?"
>
> "How strictly were you raised?"
>
> "When did you get your first job?"
>
> "What do you feel were the effects of your early home influences?"

The purpose of these questions is to provide the interviewer with insight into the early influences of your childhood. Those influences can provide clues as to whether or not your development was normal. The interviewer will be looking for any unusual advantages or disadvantages you may have encountered. Because it's almost impossible for anyone to predict the effect of childhood influences, the interviewer may not be able to make any assumptions about you that are valid. It is the invalid assumptions, however, that we're concerned with.

If you have any skeletons in your family closet, keep them there. The interview session is not a forum to air dirty linen. If your father was the town drunk who beat up your mother regularly, keep the information to yourself. Tell it to your psychiatrist, not your potential employer. Even if your father has only one positive attribute, use that one attribute to describe him. Build it up, embellish it, and make him into a superdad.

Everything else you reveal about your early childhood should indicate positive influences on your development. So what if you didn't have a paying job at age fourteen. You did chores around the house; you washed the family car; you cut the grass; you ran errands. You did a lot of positive things that molded you into the person you are today. Tell the interviewer those positive events from your early childhood; make him or her envy you.

Education

> "Tell me about your education after graduating from high school"
>
> "How did you happen to go to college?"
>
> "When did you choose your college major?"
>
> "Have you ever changed your major interest in college? Why?"
>
> "What courses did you like best? Which least? Why?"
>
> "Do you feel you've done the best scholastic work you're capable of?"

"What percentage of your college expenses did you earn? How?"

"What extracurricular activities did you participate in? What offices did you hold?"

"What were your grades in college? Were they average, above average, or below average?"

"What were your scores on your Scholastic Aptitude Tests?"

The interviewer, by delving into your educational background, can gain considerable insight into your ability, your personality, and your motivation. Your ability can be determined by analyzing your likes and dislikes. Interests tend to correlate with abilities. If you indicate an interest in scientific matters, then chances are you have an aptitude for work of a technical nature. If you have a preference for verbal subjects such as history or languages, you will have indicated strong clues for a job requiring communicating ability.

Subject dislikes will provide clues about your limitations. If, for example, you state that you dislike mathematics, the interviewer may interpret that to mean that you either have little aptitude for math or that you failed to study hard enough to awaken your interest in it. If you indicate a dislike for any subject, you will be asked, "Why?" If the subject is closely related to the requirements of the job, then you must be prepared to deal with it effectively. You might, for example, reveal the progress you've made in that subject since college. You can describe your on-the-job proficiency or your self-study progress or any additional training or education that you've had in the subject. If you haven't done anything to improve or overcome your past deficiencies, you should be able to describe the future efforts you plan to make in that area. If you're thinking of taking a course at a nearby college or of attending seminars, say so.

If the question of grades comes up, you should be prepared to identify the major factors responsible for your grade level, be it high or low. If you earned high grades, the interviewer will problably conclude that you have both intellect and motivation. If you earned only average grades, the interviewer will try to determine one of two possibilities. The first possibility is that you're bright but didn't apply yourself; so you only worked hard enough to get by. The second possibility is that you're not too bright; so you worked hard and did the best you could. The second case is more favorable then the first in terms of motivation and hard work; however, the first case is more favorable in terms of intellect. Your answer should indicate that you possessed more intellect than motivation. If you had it to do over again, you would definitely do better, because you'd be more motivated. A lack of motivation is easier to explain than a lack of intellect. Therefore, pin the rap on motivation, and let your intellect come shining through. If you received poor grades, you may have worked hard but were unable to come up with anything better. Or the school may have been very tough, and you were simply in over your head. Whatever the reason, your answer should stress the fact that since college, you have continued to improve your knowledge and ability and that in nonacademic ways, you have been successful.

What you lack in intellectual ability is more than offset by hard work and dedication. You should demonstrate a willingness to dig into problems and stay with them until they are solved. In short, you want to get across to the interviewer that your work habits and life experiences more than compensate for your academic record.

If you're asked about the scores from your high school Scholastic Aptitude Tests, then you should be prepared to discuss the results. Again, if your scores were high, you'll encounter no problem. If they were low on either the verbal ability portion or the numerical portion, then be prepared to defend the low scores with whatever reason you feel comfortable with. Perhaps you were sick that day, or you froze up during the tests. College interviewers will generally ask about SATs. Your SAT scores help them further evaluate your intelligence and aptitude. Anyone out of school for two or three years will most likely not be asked about SATs.

Job history

"Tell me about the jobs you have held since college."

"How were they obtained?"

"Why did you leave?"

"Tell me about your present job."

"What do you consider your major responsibilities in your last job?"

"In your last job, what were some of the things you spent the most time doing?"

"What things do you feel you did particularly well?"

"What things did you have difficulty with?"

"What was the reason for leaving your last job? What about the one before that?"

Your job history along with the reasons for leaving your past jobs, are two of the most important and sensitive areas that will be explored during the interview. The interviewer is going to be persistent in questioning you in this area. He or she will use every technique we discussed. This includes direct questions, open-ended questions, reflection and interpretation. You'll be asked to clarify and elaborate on your responses. The interviewer will loop back and constantly test for inconsistencies in your answers. Why? Because the reasons behind job changes can tell an interviewer more about a candidate than anything else. You can be looking for a new job, because you're just out of college, or you just got fired, or you want more money or challenge or responsibility. Whatever the reason, you must furnish a good one for each position, or you may be knocked out of the box and dropped from further consideration.

Some good, solid reasons for leaving a job are: money, challenge, opportunity, a more prestigious company, advancement, increased responsibility, geographic preference. Some questionable reasons are: personality conflict, reduction-in-force, reorganization, lack of opportunity, no room for growth, mutually satisfactory release. Some unacceptable reasons are: conflict with a superior, termination for cause, ineptitude for job, failure to perform work, medical reasons (more about this later), early retirement.

In formulating your answers, make sure you come up with acceptable reasons even if you have to stretch the truth or rationalize the real reasons away in your own mind. To further cover your tracks, only furnish references from individuals who will support your reasons. In the event the prospective employer decides to confirm your story, it should check out. I'm not recommending that you deliberately construct falsehoods. What I am suggesting is that you assess all the facts that contributed to your voluntary or involuntary termination and articulate only that portion that favors you. True, you may have to commit a sin of omission, but keep in mind, the employer may not be telling the exact truth either when describing the reasons why the job is open. It could be that you're applying for a job your predecessor left in pure disgust because of the working conditions. Make up your story, then stick to it. Sharp interviewers know that it takes two or three good reasons for people to change jobs; so you should have at least three convincing reasons for leaving each job. Money, challenge, and opportunity are excellent. They must be articulated in such a manner, however, that it doesn't make you come across as an opportunist or a job hopper, completely devoid of loyalty or gratitude toward your past employers.

How did you feel about your job?

"What are some of the problems you encountered?"

"What frustrates you the most?"

"What do you do about those frustrations?"

"How do you feel about the progress you've made with your present company?"

"How have you developed in your job?"

"What has been your greatest frustration or disappointment in your present job, and why do you feel this way?"

"What are some of the reasons you had for leaving your last job?"

"What is your general impression of the last company you worked for?"

"What did you like about your last job?"

"What were some of the minuses in your last job?

"Do you consider your progress on the job representative of your ability? Why?"

"Compared to your other jobs, how do you rank your last one? Why?"

"How many hours a week do you feel a person should devote to a job?"

Your feelings about your current job and your past jobs will provide clues for the interviewer that can point up your strengths or your shortcomings. The interviewer might formulate a hypothesis about you that says you're not telling the truth about how you feel about your past jobs and, moreover, that you structured your remarks to hide those facts. Your job is to convince the interviewer that you *are* telling the truth and that your reasons are genuine. You can accomplish this by sticking to your story, being consistent, and not contradicting yourself.

How do you feel about people?

"Describe your supervisor to me."

"What are some of the things you and your supervisor disagreed about?"

"What do you feel were your supervisor's greatest strengths?"

"What areas do you feel your supervisor could have improved upon?"

"How do you feel about the way your supervisor treated you and the others in your department?"

"How has your supervisor helped you to develop?"

"What are some things your supervisor did that you liked? How about those you disliked?"

"Do you feel your supervisor rated you fairly? Can you support that conclusion?"

"What did your supervisor rate you the highest on?"

"What criticism did your supervisor make of your work? How did you feel about that conclusion?"

"What kind of people do you like to work with?"

"What kind of people do you find it most difficult to work with?"

"Have you been successful in working with people you dislike? How do you do it?"

Your attitude toward others and your interpersonal relations are of extreme importance in evaluating you as a potential employee. An individual can be the brightest, hardest working, technically competent, and productive employee in the world; but if he or she can't get along with other people—be they peers, subordinates, or superiors—then that individual is doomed to the rejection pile. Good interpersonal skills and good human relations are essential for success. Few, if any, jobs can be performed in a void without interacting with others. By asking the above questions, the interviewer, is trying to gather data that will tell him or her how you feel about others. Your responses must indicate that your relations have always been good and that you have never encountered any problems in this area.

If you have had problems here, then once again play

them down and accent only the positive factors. Telling an interviewer that you have personal relations problems is one red flag that will wave you out of consideration. The interviewer should believe that your ability to get along with others is superior, that you create good will and warm, friendly feelings with everyone you come in contact with. With subordinates, you are firm but fair; with peers, you give and take; with superiors, you take direction and guidance in a positive manner. You rarely antagonize anyone, and you're known for your ability to get along well with everyone. Don't overdo it, but answer this line of questioning thoughtfully.

Job objectives

> "Why do you feel you would like to work for our company?"
>
> "What are some of the things in a job that are important to you, and why?"
>
> "What are some of the things in a job you dislike, and why?"
>
> "Aside from money, what do you want from your next job that you're not getting from your present job?"
>
> "What is your overall career objective?"
>
> "What are you doing to reach that objective?"
>
> "What is your salary expectation?"
>
> "How did you arrive at that figure?"
>
> "What do you consider satisfactory earnings progression from this point?"

The interviewer realizes you don't know where you want to be five years from now or ten years from now. What the interviewer wants to know, however, is whether you're drifting along with the tide like a ship without a rudder, or whether you have thought through your career objectives in a meaningful, purposeful way. Are your goals realistic? Can they be achieved? What are your time frames? Can you accomplish your objectives in the time allotted? Or are you throwing up a big smoke screen?

In answering these questions, display solid thinking backed up by evidence you can produce—if required. If challenge or responsibility are important to you in a job, then you must be able to give examples of how much responsibility you had in past jobs or how you successfully met past challenges. If you do dislike certain elements in a job, you must be able to convince the interviewer that you had good and sufficient reasons for your dislikes and that you were not alone in your feelings.

Your self-image

"Describe yourself."

"What do you consider to be your greatest strength?"

"What about your weaknesses?"

"What traits do you feel you can most improve upon?"

"Are there certain things you feel more confident in doing than others? What are they? Why do you feel that way?"

"What are some of the things that motivate you?"

"Without naming him (her), think of your best friend.
    Describe that friend."
"How are you alike? How do you differ?"
"What are your hobbies?"
"What do you read?"
"How do you spend your free time?"

During the course of the interview, you should project
an image of enthusiasm, ambition, confidence, maturity,
and sound judgment. You'll need to project an image that
is in line with each situation. Almost always, you'll need to
project an image of honesty, sincerity, dedication to
achievement, a high energy level, and that of a likeable
person. You will also be required to project parts of your
image that meet the criteria or hiring standards of the
specific position you're applying for.

In describing yourself, do so in a manner that has a
touch of modesty, yet highlights your strengths. In describing your weaknesses, turn them around so they come
out as strengths. For example, my greatest weakness is my
inability to leave my work at the office; but in describing it,
I could project it as a strength by emphasizing its bearing
on my involvement with my work.

In describing what motivates you, select a few topics
that would motivate most successful people. For example,
achieving tough goals or objectives, overcoming difficult
problems, increasing productivity, gaining on the competition, and so forth.

Always be prepared to say something that can tie in
your past achievements to some potential problem area in
the job you're interviewing for. Then describe how your
past, relevant experiences can be brought to bear on your
new challenges.

Conditions of work

"Do you like to travel?"

"How do you feel about overtime work?"

"Do you prefer a large or small company? Why?"

"Are you willing to go where the company sends you?"

"Are you able to relocate? At company expense? At your own expense?"

"What are your geographical preferences?"

Condition-of-work questions are pretty straightforward. Your answers should indicate that you're willing to perform all aspects of the job and that you have no preferences strong enough to restrict your candidacy for the position. If you *do* have strong feelings about relocation, overtime, geographical areas or size of company, don't express them! After you get the job offer, you'll have plenty of time to weigh the pros and cons. If the cons outweigh the pros, then you can always reject the offer. In other words, don't erect any barriers prior to the offer of employment. You can always reject the offer or, at the very least, negotiate once you have been made an offer.

Miscellaneous questions

"Can you get recommendations from previous employers?"

"Have you had any serious illness or injury?"

"Tell me about your military service."

"Are you primarily interested in money, or do you feel service to humanity is a concern?"

"Define *cooperation*."

It's impossible to spell out every conceivable question that may come up during an interview, so be prepared for anything. In the next chapter, more of these questions are categorized for you.

9

Where will you be five years from now?

One day a friend and I were talking, and the subject of interviewing questions came up. My friend, also in personnel, argued that the question, "Where do you expect to be five years from now?" wasn't a very good one. He gave several reasons to support his viewpoint. First of all, he claimed, no one really knows where they'll be or hope to be five years from now. Secondly, most candidates would provide you with an answer that showed they'd be promoted and most likely be high up in the organization in a responsible position.

I agreed with him on both points. However, I disagreed on the value of the question itself. I've always used that question to set the stage for the second and third questions in order to get deeper into the subject. For example, I ask, "Where do you expect to be five years from now?" Then I follow up with, "And what are you doing to prepare yourself for that position?" And, "What if you don't achieve your goal?" To win in a job interview, you must be prepared to deal with this line of in-depth questioning.

The following examples should help you to prepare for in-depth questions. As you read them, formulate your own responses. I've divided them into distinct categories, so that you can focus on one area at a time. Let's begin with your work pattern.

Work pattern

Tell me about your work history.
How did you happen to get the job?
I'd be interested in knowing the kinds of work you did.
Would you explain your reason(s) for leaving?
Tell me more about what you found disappointing
or frustrating in your work.
Would you explain why?
Would you tell me about what criticism was made of your
work by your employers?
I'm not certain I understand what kind of criticism.
To what do you attribute the criticism?
I'm be interested in knowing what is most important
to you in a job.
Would you explain what you care least about in a job?
What do you mean by that?
Tell me about your usual reaction when called down by a
superior for doing something wrong.
If you were in a position to make changes on your previous
jobs, *tell me* what you would have done.
Would you explain that in more detail?
How do you feel about relocating and travel away from home?
Perhaps you could clarify . . . when would you be
able to relocate?

Educational and social pattern

Tell me about your scholastic performance in college. In other schools?

What was there about the extracurricular activities you participated in *that appealed to you*, and what offices did you hold in high school? In college?

Has there been an opportunity for you to earn a portion of your educational expenses?

What prompted your decision to do that?

Would you tell me about the experience during your school days that stands out as meaning the most to you?

To what do you attribute the importance of that experience?

Would you explain how old you were when you earned your first money on a steady job?

How did you happen to do that?

Tell me about your participation in outside activities.

Personality

Would you tell me about what you believe to be your strong points as a person?

What do you mean by that?

I'd be interested in knowing what you believe to be your weak points as a person.

What do you mean by that?

Would you tell me about qualities you admire in other people?

Perhaps you could clarify why you admire these qualities.

Tell me about what irritates or displeases you most in other people.

I'd be interested in knowing about the last incident that made you angry.

Would you explain what you did about it?

95

Ambitions

I'd be interested in knowing what position you want to hold several years from now.
Would you tell me about why you believe you will be qualified for that position?
I'm not certain I understand your plans to qualify yourself.
Tell me about the reputation you like to enjoy as an employee.
What do you mean by that?
What prompted your decision to apply for this job with our company?
Would you explain why we should hire you?

Granted, these are tough questions, but I've revealed the strategy behind such queries and suggested possible answers in the Appendix.

10

Are you one of a protected class?

A number of questions should *not* be, but sometimes are, asked of women and members of minority groups. Certain groups of people in the United States have suffered the effects of discrimination in employment. The federal government has identified these groups and labeled them "protected classes." Protected classes are defined as those who have suffered and continue to suffer the effects of discrimination. These are blacks, women, persons between the ages of 40 and 65 (and older, pending legislation that will raise the limit to 70 years of age), Spanish-surnamed persons, American Indians, handicapped persons (both mentally and physically), Asian–Americans (including Filipinos) and Latin Americans (including Puerto Ricans, Mexican–Americans, Cubans, and Spanish–Americans).

Various federal laws, state laws, and executive orders legislate equal opportunity. In addition, there are agencies at the federal and state levels that enforce this legislation. These agencies, however, do not publish guides on pre-employment inquiries, so it is difficult to categorize any particular interview question as legal or illegal. The federal government can, however, request proof that any questions used during an interview are job related and therefore are necessary to the screening of applicants and not used for a discriminatory purpose.

I've compiled a list of questions I consider to be improper. If you're a member of a protected class and these questions are asked of you, you may find yourself in a predicament. Here's why: If you duck the questions, you may not get the job. If you answer the questions unfavorably, you may be discriminated against and not get the job; but if you answer the questions favorably, you may get the job. Whatever the outcome, if you feel you were discriminated against, you may have grounds to file a complaint with the Equal Employment Opportunity Commission (EEOC) or, if warranted, to institute a lawsuit. Although that course of action is outside the scope of this book, I'd recommend you answer the questions carefully. Your objective is to land the job.

Most likely, you'll not be subjected to answering such improper questions if the interviewer is in tune with the law. In large corporations, the interviewer usually will be knowledgeable about the law and will refrain from asking job applicants improper questions. Occasionally, however, you may encounter an unenlightened individual who will ask you one of the following questions. If this happens, answer judiciously. Although I've furnished answers you can use, several questions require answers only you can formulate.

Questions directed at women

Marital relations

Q. Why aren't you married?
A. I haven't found the right person.

Q. Do you plan to get married?
A. Yes, when the right person comes along.

Q. If you get married, would you continue your career?
A. My marital status would not affect my career.

Q. Does your husband object to your working late?
A. My husband and I agree on many things, and one of those is doing a job to the best of one's ability.

Q. Are you able to travel?
A. Yes.

Q. Are you able to relocate?
A. Yes, providing it's a location that's agreeable to my family.

Child rearing

Q. Do you have any children?
A. Yes or no.

Q. Do you plan to have any?
A. That's a decision that has to be made carefully by my husband and me.

Q. What ages are your children?
A. Answer accordingly.

Q. Who baby-sits your children while you work?
A. Answer accordingly.

Q. Do you think your children get good care while you are working?

A. Yes. Our concern as parents and the quality of our child care more than meets their needs.

Personal finances

Q. Do you get alimony?

A. Yes, the need for that has been substantiated and taken care of.

Q. Do you get child support?

A. Yes, the need for that has been substantiated and taken care of.

Miscellaneous

Q. Are you a member of any women's liberation organization?

A. No, or yes, in order to help promote a long overdue advancement of women.

Q. Do men find it distracting to work with you?

A. I'm such a diligent worker that most people are busy trying to keep up with me.

Questions directed at blacks

Q. Do you have a car?

A. Yes; or no, but I have never encountered any difficulty in getting to and from work.

Q. Do you own your own home?

A. Yes; or no, but it has always been my dream to one day own a home.

Q. Have you ever had your salary garnisheed?

A. No; or yes, but it won't happen again.

Q. What kind of discharge did you get from the armed forces?

A. Answer accordingly. If other than honorable, say: I've had to work twice as hard to overcome the stigma of my discharge, and I feel my efforts prove that I'm more responsible now than I was in my younger days in the Army when I was just out of high school.

Questions directed at people over 40

Q. We're a fast-paced outfit. Do you find that you have trouble keeping up these days?

A. No.

Q. How's your record for getting to work on time?

A. It's never been a problem.

Q. What's a typical workday for you like?

A. I'm more productive now than ever. Also, I'm working a lot smarter than I used to, and I get better results from my efforts.

Q. Are you collecting any retirement, pension, or disability payments?

A. Answer accordingly.

Questions asked of Spanish-surnamed people and Asian–Americans

Q. Where were you born?

A. Answer accordingly.

Q. Where were your spouse and parents born?

A. Answer accordingly.

Q. Will you provide names of three relatives other than your father, husband, wife, or minor-age, dependent children?

A. Yes.

Q. Where did you learn to speak a foreign language?

A. Answer accordingly.

Questions asked of American Indians

Q. Do you receive any money from the federal government?

A. Answer accordingly.

Q. Why do you want to work?

A. To earn a living for myself and my family.

The importance of answering these questions tactfully, without showing signs of hostility or annoyance, no matter how offensive the questions may be, cannot be overemphasized. It's always preferable to maintain rapport between yourself and your interviewer. If you feel you were asked improper questions and that you were indeed discriminated against, then by all means contact the EEOC; but keep calm during the interview. The purpose of this book is to help you win that job, and you stand your best chance of doing that by walking a tightrope when it comes to answering improper and sometimes offensive questions that don't seem to be job related.

Developing your own interview strategy

As we saw in Chapter 1, the interviewer has four objectives. These are getting started, gathering facts and insights that will allow him or her to predict your future performance, stimulating interest by explaining and perhaps selling the position to you, and closing the interview. Let's take a look now at what some of *your* objectives should be during the interview.

- You should present yourself in the most favorable light, and sell yourself to the interviewer.
- Gather as much information as you can about the position and the organization so that you can make a decision about the company.
- Develop other objectives to fit your own personal needs.

In trying to achieve your objectives, you should be aware of the fact that interviewing is more an art than a science. Because it is an art, there can be a poor correlation between what the interviewer evaluates and predicts about you and what you can actually do. This inability to predict future performance based on the interview is generally broken down into three categories: external factors, personal qualifications of the interviewer, and the method used to evaluate candidates after the interview is concluded. In developing your strategy, be alert to weaknesses of the interview process; and exploit these weaknesses to your advantage!

External factors

If you were interviewed after an impressive candidate, then the interviewer will tend to evaluate you somewhat less favorably than if you followed a weak candidate. Also, appearance is important. Applicants who are overweight or sloppily dressed are less likely to be hired than those with comparable qualifications who make a good appearance. Remember—you're being compared to others. So in order to win, you must score better than they do in as many categories as possible.

That all-important
first impression

Many interviewers tend to hire in their own image. They have preconceived notions of what the ideal candidate should be. As a result, they enter the interview situation with biases that cause them to evaluate applicants as total human beings with human frailties as opposed to job-related deficiencies. This is further complicated by the overpowering tendency to make a complete evaluation of a candidate early in the interview, often from the impression formed in the first two or three minutes. This initial impression is often based on information that is totally unrelated to job performance. For example, it may be dress, bearing, firmness of handshake, hair style, facial expression, or other physical characteristics.

Your attitude will have an influence on how you're initially judged. Are you open-minded to change? Will you be a teamworker? Will you be cooperative? Will you fit in with other members of the company in terms of your ability to work well with others and not cause any personality conflicts? Will you come across as a well set-up, healthy, energetic person with good bodily and facial characteristics? Will you be perceived as being well groomed, with an erect posture, or slouchy and unattractive in appearance? Will your voice impress the interviewer as being irritating or pleasant? Are you perceived as one whose judgment will be dependable even under stress; or will you impress the interviewer as being hasty, erratic, biased, or easily swayed emotionally?

For example, your responses to the interviewer's questions may provide evidence that you have acquired the habit of making considered judgments. You weigh the pros and cons of a situation before you render any judgmental decision. On the other hand, a tendency to react impulsively and without restraint in answering questions that require judgment will lose points for you.

Another key element in creating a good first impression is to present yourself as an emotionally stable individual. To do that, you must appear well poised. If you are by nature touchy, sensitive to criticism, or easily upset, strive instead for coolness and restraint. Once judged as "easily irritated," or "impatient," or "oversensitive," or "easily disconcerted," you'll be out of consideration. Picture yourself as poised and in control.

Another key element of that first impression is your level of self-confidence. If you seem to be uncertain of yourself, easily bluffed, overly self-conscious, or timid, your impact as a candidate will be negative. You must impress the interviewer as one who is self-confident and assured.

Once the interviewer forms a first impression of you, he or she will tend to seek out and interpret information that reinforces that initial impression. All too often, it's difficult—if not impossible—to overcome the stigma of a bad first impression. Think of the interviewer as the buyer in a buyer/seller relationship. If you impress the interviewer from the beginning, he or she will treat you as if you're already an employee. You'll perceive this as the interviewer answers your questions fully and thoroughly or shares a lot of company information on benefits. In general, the interviewer will try to sell you, the candidate, on the attractiveness of the company. On the other hand, if the interviewer tries to sell you off the company, or does not provide adequate answers to your questions, or tries to tell you that you may be better qualified for a job other than the one for which you're being interviewed, you can bet you haven't impressed the interviewer. When you perceive this, muster your wits and work twice as hard to reverse that first impression and overcome it. To win, you must make the most of that first impression! You must also make good on it by being able to follow through and deliver.

Determination of a professional
interviewing team

If you undergo two or more successive interviews with the same company, you may detect a pattern. In order to overcome the unreliability of the interview process and to diminish the influence of the factors that contribute to that unreliability, the seasoned, professional, interviewing team will have accomplished two things. First, they will have designed a patterned interview; and second, they will have developed a selection strategy. The patterned interview ensures that the interviewers are covering the job-related areas of information and that they are doing it consistently. This results in their being able to gather data without injecting their own personal biases. The development of a selection strategy ensures that all interviewers in the hiring process are looking for the same candidate. They will have defined very carefully what the ideal candidate will look like in terms of experience, education, and personal qualities and characteristics. This combination of the patterned interview and the development of a selection strategy enables them to remove many of the unreliable factors from the interview situation.

If, on the other hand, the interviewers interview you in completely different styles and ask you questions unrelated to each other, if they pursue different subjects—then you know that they most likely haven't been trained. If you're qualified, without a doubt, for the position and you find yourself in the hands of a professional, then you stand an excellent chance of getting the position. On the other hand, if you're well qualified and find yourself the subject of an uncoordinated recruiting effort, then you must recognize it as such. Try to furnish data and information that will lead each successive interviewer to believe that you're the ideal candidate for the job. This can be accomplished if you're sensitive to the personal needs of the interviewer and respond to those needs.

If you feel, by the line of questioning, that the interviewer is definitely interested in you, then you must maintain that level of interest. If, however, the interviewer asks you a question and lets you ramble on and you sense the interviewer is not listening to your responses, then you must regain his or her interest and keep the interview on track. This can be done by asking the interviewer a question at the appropriate time that will respark the interview and give you additional clues as to how your future responses should be made. This technique is intended to enable you to make the most favorable review from each interviewer in the loop.

Remember—to win, you must sell each and every interviewer in the process. Two out of three or three out of four is not good enough. Any one of them can blackball you. Don't be misled by the size of the office or the title of each person in the hiring loop. Each one has a vital role in selection and is there for the express purpose of evaluating you! Be at your best with each, and make your answers consistent.

Watch out for a probing strategy

As you go from interviewer to interviewer, each may be sharing information they have obtained from you. If you did not make yourself clear or if you have not satisfied one interviewer, he or she will most likely ask the next interviewer to "probe" more deeply into the subject. To win, you must convince the succeeding interviewer that you are prepared and capable of giving satisfactory answers.

12

Spell the name of the company correctly

The number of errors applicants make is unlimited. They range from simple errors such as mispronuncing a word or phrase to such gross, tactical errors as positioning oneself as an upper-level manager for a position that requires a shirt-sleeve, hands-on professional. I know one personnel manager who systematically eliminates candidates who, in letters of application, spell his name or his company's name wrong. I've detailed a number of pitfalls you can avoid if you are aware of them and understand them.

Be able to state your own worth

Invariably, the subject of money will come up during the interview. From your employment application, résumé, extensive questioning, the interviewer will have a pretty good knowledge of your past salary history. He or she will now want to know *what* your salary requirement is and *why* it is what it is. When you're asked about your salary requirement, you must be able to state your worth. You must not equivocate or use such expressions as, "It would be *nice* to get X amount of dollars," or, "I was *hoping* to be paid such and such." Your statement should be, "Based on my knowledge, experience, and track record, my salary requirement is X dollars." If the company tries to negotiate you downward or offers you a lower amount, reject it. If they want you, they'll usually pay you your asking price. Sound companies don't nickel-and-dime people they want to hire. In fact, the opposite is generally true. They will want to ensure that they're offering enough not only to attract you but to bring you on board with a highly motivated attitude.

Welcome change and forget about job security

Don't ask the interviewer questions about benefits, layoffs, turnover, or any other subject that indicates you're looking for security. If those things are important to you, then ask someone else in the company. It's fairly easy to gather that kind of information over the phone, simply by calling the personnel department. Instead, indicate a high level of confidence in yourself as a person more interested in change and challenge than anything else. The applicant who fares the best is the one who displays more concern about the company's welfare than about his or her own welfare. Pay, benefits, and other aspects of jobs are by-products, not prerequisites, of success; they don't motivate the truly productive worker. Rather, the job and its challenge are the driving forces. Throughout the interview, you'd be better off to indicate a strong need for change and challenge. Forget about job security; it's an illusion, anyway. The only real security is your own ability.

Develop rapport quickly and get rid of the interview jitters

The more quickly you create a warm, amiable feeling between you and the interviewer, the faster you'll be able to be yourself. If you fail to develop rapport quickly, you'll probably be nervous and unable to express yourself as well as you might when you're more relaxed. Naturally, most people will be somewhat anxious going into an interview. This is normal and to be expected. If the nervousness persists, however, it can be detrimental to the outcome of your interview. The more self-assurance you project, the more credibility you'll establish. For example, if you're telling the interviewer how well you accomplished a certain task or how you met a difficult objective while you're acting in a manner indicative of a low level of self-confidence, then your words won't ring true. Your credibility will be a question mark in the interviewer's mind.

One way to overcome the interview jitters is by thorough preparation. You've already taken a step in that direction by reading this book. The next step is to discover as much as you can about your interviewer, the job vacancy, and the company. In preparing, you may actually reach the point where you will be looking forward to the interview. If you've done your homework, you will be anxious to get in there and do your stuff.

Don't confuse a job interview
with a guidance-counseling session

On more occasions than I care to remember, I've started out to interview a job candidate and have ended up providing guidance counseling.

In today's job market, most positions are specialized. Employers are seeking people who can fill specific requirements. The easiest way for a candidate to get knocked out of the box is by expressing a preference for a position other than the one the interviewer is seeking to fill. One candidate said to me, "Although I'm interested in your accounts payable position, do you have anything open in advertising?" Another said, "It's true that I have a solid background in marketing, but lately I've been leaning more and more towards public relations. Do you have any openings in your public relations department?"

Obviously, if you express a preference for any job other than the one you've been brought in for, you can forget it. The employer is looking for the one person who not only meets the specifications but expresses a solid, genuine interest in putting all of his or her attention, energy, and enthusiasm into the position for which he or she is interviewing.

On another level, I have interviewed people who simply did not know what they wanted to do. So many times I've heard the question, "Well, what have you got open?" I've been afraid to answer for fear that I'd find a candidate on my hands who would apply for any job that happened to be open. Such candidates give the appearance of not thinking through their career goals; they are not likely to be hired for any meaningful position.

You must present yourself as one who views the open

position as the only job of interest to you. If you're applying for a secretarial position, then you're not interested in
being a receptionist or a clerk typist or a key punch
operator. You're a secretary; you want to work as a secretary, and nothing else is acceptable. Your stated objective
and unwavering career interest will demonstrate to the
interviewer that he or she is interviewing a prospective
employee with success potential. Why?—because you know
what you want, and you're willing to devote yourself to
achieving it.

Make sure you're understood

Don't leave any of your statements or answers open to the
wrong interpretation. If you feel that your answer to a
question could be misinterpreted, then by all means clear it
up.

Once I asked a candidate to describe a typical workday
for me. She told me that she started work at 9:00 A.M. and
promptly left at 5:00. Earlier in the interview, she had told
me that one of her key strengths was that she didn't work
by the clock and that she usually worked as many hours as
it took to get the job done. I interpreted her latter statement
as a contradiction of her earlier one. I also assumed that
once she left the office, she ceased working. The true situation was that she belonged to a car pool and had to
adhere to the car pool schedule. She did, in fact, take work
home with her, and she spent as many hours as were required to complete her work. The erroneous assumption
on my part was due to my failure to probe deeper into her
work habits. The burden was on her, however, to make
certain that she communicated that vital bit of information

in a manner that did not leave any room for a misunderstanding. If you're given the opportunity to say something positive about yourself, make sure that it's clear to your interviewer.

An interview is not a confessional

Don't under any circumstances tell the interviewer about your weaknesses, bad habits, poor health, past failures, or any other derogatory information. If you're asked about your weaknesses, you should provide an answer that describes them in such a manner that they can be construed as strengths. For example, one of your weaknesses might be a low tolerance for people who don't take their jobs seriously. You get annoyed when an employee fails to answer a telephone, or treats a customer poorly, or arrives at work late and leaves early. The interviewer will view this "weakness" as a strength. Any bad habits or past failures should remain in your own consciousness. The interview situation is your opportunity to show yourself off at your best. It's no time to lay your throbbing psyche out on the table.

Don't be a passive dependent

The interviewer knows that he or she is in the driver's seat. After all, you're selling, and the interviewer is buying. If the interviewer takes advantage of this situation and tries to ride roughshod over you, don't let him or her do it. You can control the situation by asking a few questions. By making the interviewer respond, you balance the situation. A good interviewer will respect you for the way in which you make him or her perform. It is an indication of confidence, aggressiveness, and intelligence.

How did I do, coach?

Don't ask the interviewer how you did after the interview. This could be interpreted as a lack of confidence on your part. No interviewer will tell you the straight story, anyway; so don't ask!

I really need this job

Don't appear overanxious or desperate for the job. Even if you haven't worked for some time, you must indicate that you're looking around for the best opportunity. If you give off signals that you're desperate, the interviewer will interpret them to mean that no one else is interested in you; so why should he or she be interested in you? In other words, what's wrong with this candidate? Do other personnel people know something I don't? On the other hand, if you appear to have several irons in the fire or even an offer or two in hand or on the way, the interviewer will view you as a hot commodity. He or she better act fast before someone else makes you an offer you can't refuse.

Integrity is important

Don't, under any circumstances, break the confidence of your past employer. If you do, you'll be viewed as lacking in integrity. If you're asked questions that involve proprietary information or other private company data, you must gracefully refuse to discuss it. Your refusal will enhance your position, and the interviewer will respect you all the more.

Character assasination is a no-no

Don't engage in any character assassination or demean any past supervisor, employer, or company official. Regardless of how you really feel, you should always speak well of others. If you speak ill of others, you'll be perceived as someone who may have interpersonal problems and who probably is a risk. By speaking well of everyone, you'll be judged as someone who possesses a healthy outlook in terms of others' strengths and weaknesses.

13

What to do after the interview

There are many ways to follow up after the interview or series of interviews. You can do it by telephone, through your employment agency, in person, or by letter. I recommend you do follow up in writing and that your letter serve as a vehicle to enhance your candidacy. Whatever you do, it must work to your advantage and not vice versa. Before we get into the contents of a good follow-up letter, let's take a look at some of the things you *shouldn't* do.

First of all, don't "bug" the recruiter or the interviewer. The company needs time to make a hiring decision; it will probably be interviewing many candidates over a period of time in order to hire the best person. Often I've interviewed candidates who called back the next day, wanting to know where they stood. I admit that it's difficult to go home and wait, but you should realize that it takes time to make a hiring decision. A postinterview phone call will most likely only irritate the interviewer. When and if they're going to make you an offer, they'll call you. The old "don't call us, we'll call you" bromide applies.

A more professional approach is to write the interviewer a letter. In the case of multiple interviews, multiple letters—all slightly different—should be written. The letters should be constructed to accomplish a number of objectives. First of all, they should be on crisp, clean paper, neatly and accurately written or typed, properly addressed with the recipient's name and title correctly spelled, and on your own stationery—not your past or present employer's. The body of the letter should express your interest in the position, your positive assessment of the company and its people, your qualifications for the opening, and your intention to accept the job if offered. Below is a good example of what a follow-up letter should be. I recommend you send out a similar letter after each interview.

Dear Mr. _____:

Since our meeting of (date), I have given a great deal of thought to the prospects of a career with (company name) and would like to go on record as saying that I am keenly interested in the exceptional opportunity presented to me at that time.

I was impressed by the dynamic growth of your company, the caliber of your management team, and the nature and scope of the products we discussed.

I believe I have the necessary qualifications for the position.
1. A college degree—Honors, and so forth
2. A successful background in (field of expertise).
3. Important business contacts
4. A particular interest in the application of your product to the market place

I am anticipating a favorable decision by your company with respect to the particular opening. I ask only for the opportunity to join your staff at this time, knowing that ability, competence, and proven performance will be recognized and rewarded in the long run.

As you suggested, I will be contacting you by telephone (date), regarding your decision.

Sincerely,

John Doe

This kind of follow-up letter is another tool that can give you the competitive edge. Use it!

14

Your scenario for success

The initial interview with the company is designed to provide the interviewer with information on your life story: your employment history, education, experience, health, and so forth. Subsequent interviews will delve more deeply into your personal attributes and characteristics.

Finally, the company will make a judgment based on its perceptions as to the probability of your being the best person for the position and the one who has the highest probability for success. When they choose you over the other applicants, you'll be offered the job. I hope I've helped you increase your chances toward that end.

APPENDIX

What the interviewer's question really means

Personnel people have their own code questions. In other words, the questions we ask you may sound innocent enough, but there's a definite purpose to them. On the following pages, I've listed twenty frequently asked questions, what we're really looking for when we ask them, and some suggested strategies for answering them.

1. "How did you happen to get into this line of work?"

REALLY MEANS: "Did you assess your likes and dislikes before making a choice? Or did you fall into your present line of work? Did you methodically seek out a career field that matched your aptitude, ability, or interest? Or were you forced into your career field out of economic necessity?" Usually, people doing the kind of work they like best make the best employees.

Frequently, I've interviewed applicants looking for an economic opportunity rather than a job that makes the best use of their abilities. I've talked to applicants with college degrees who wanted a secretarial or receptionist job. The reason usually given is "to get a foot in the door." Then, a year or two later, when they haven't moved up the corporate ladder, they experience job frustration. For this reason, I only hire secretaries who want to remain secretaries.

If an interviewer asks you this question, you must make a choice. Either you really are happy in your line of work and can give logical reasons for being in it; or you can furnish a plausible reason for doing the kind of work you do, and you have an even better reason now for getting out of it.

2. *"What percentage of your college expenses did you earn?"*

REALLY MEANS: "Are you a self-made person, or have opportunities been served up to you on a silver platter?" If you did pay part or all of your tuition, let it be known. If you didn't, think back to a summer job you had—nearly everyone has had at least *one* summer job while they were going to school—and mention the money you earned from that job and how it helped pay expenses.

3. *"You seem to have had quite a few jobs. Can you explain why there's been so much change?"*

REALLY MEANS: "You look like a job hopper to me, a sign of instability. You'd better have a good explanation." If you tell me the job changes were because of "reorganization" or a "personality conflict" or "mutually agreeable separation," my red flag goes up and I become suspicious. Better answers are "a reduction in work force because of lack of work" or "better money" or "better opportunity." I still want to delve into these reasons, but I'm a lot less suspicious. In short, put the best possible light on your job changes; and if your résumé lists too many jobs, eliminate one or two and fudge some dates. Few personnel people check the veracity of every date. If there are gaps of a few months, you were probably traveling in Europe, or you came down with the mumps. Right? Right.

4. "How did past employers treat you?"

REALLY MEANS: "What kind of employee will you be? Are you the kind of person who carries a grudge, or can you be objective about situations that might have been disagreeable to you?" If, in fact, you feel you didn't get a fair shake in your previous job, resist the urge to say so. A desirable answer is, "Under the circumstances, I believe I was treated quite fairly." This kind of answer shows strength of character.

5. "Without naming him or her, think of your closest friend. Describe that person. Tell me how you and he/she differ."

REALLY MEANS: "Your best friend will give me insight into what makes you tick." If your best friend drinks his lunch at the local tavern, you probably do, too. If she's an avid tennis player, you probably spend a lot of time on the courts, too. As you answer this question, be sure to point out *positive* characteristics of your friend. Remember that a friend is a reflection on you; so he or she should be everything you deem desirable.

6. "What do you know about our company?"

REALLY MEANS: "How interested in us are you?" The more you know, the better off you'll be. Before the interview, read all the material you can about the company. Dip into *Moody's* or *Standard & Poor's*. Ask the public relations department to send you the company magazine and the annual report. You should know in general how large the company is and what it does or makes.

7. "Can you get recommendations from previous employers?"

REALLY MEANS: "What are the circumstances under which you left your last company?" If you can get recommendations that would be favorable, then simply answer, "yes." If you can't get recommendations, be prepared to answer this question in a manner that will work toward your best interests. For example, "Yes, I believe my former employer will recommend me" then hedge by adding, "but I believe they have a policy against providing information on past employees other than that of confirming employment dates."

8. "Of all the positions you have had, which did you like most? Why? Which did you like least? Why?"

REALLY MEANS: "What was your relationship with your supervisors?" As you answer the question, the interviewer will be comparing your answer to his or her characteristics. Your response should be general in nature and should point up the positive characteristics of your former supervisors. Don't make any negative comments or perform any character assassinations on previous supervisors. If you do, a red flag will go up, and the interviewer will screen you out. About the last thing they want to hire is an individual who has had problems with supervisors.

A positive approach to answering this question would be for you to stress the best characteristics of your supervisor and to relate to the interviewer the positive things that you learned from him or her. In answering the question about the things you liked least about your former supervisor, you can turn the negative factors into positive ones. Say something like, "One of the things I liked least about my supervisor was the fact that he was too easy on his subordinates. I felt that he could have gotten a lot more productivity out of me and others if he had only pushed us a little harder. Other than that, almost all of my supervisors were fair and did a good job."

9. "What types of people seem to rub you the wrong way?"

REALLY MEANS: "How do you relate with others?" In answering this question, try to define the kind of person you think would rub most people the wrong way. In other words, instead of supplying the interviewer with your subjective answer, be a little more objective. For example, most people don't like phonies. So you can tell the interviewer that you don't like "phonies." If, on the other hand, you tell the interviewer that you don't like politicians, you may have a battle on your hands. Politicians are a necessary evil, and many people have grown tolerant of them. So stick to clear-cut types that will keep you clear of any disagreements.

10. "What type of atmosphere existed at your former company?"

REALLY MEANS: "What's the best job atmosphere for you?" If the atmosphere was similar to that of the job you're interviewing for, you're in luck. However, if the atmosphere within your last company was, say, heavy on policies, demanded strict adherence to procedure and compliance to company rules and regulations, and that of the company that's interviewing you is a lot more permissive, then that kind of difference will be important for the interviewer. Here again, prior to answering the question, you should try to gain insight into the atmosphere that exists in the company. The closer you come to matching that atmosphere in your response, the better off you will be.

11. "What kind of guidance did you get from your supervisors?"

REALLY MEANS: "Are you a self-starter; do you take the initiative and work on your own? Or do you need close supervision, occasional coaching, or day–to–day guidance and control in order to do your job?" It would be definitely to your advantage to answer this question by indicating that you required little or no guidance in the performance of your duties; also, that you produced excellent results with a minimum amount of supervision.

12. "What is the nature of your typical workday?"

REALLY MEANS: "What's the amount of work you accomplish during a workday?" The interviewer wants to know what your energy level is—exactly what you accomplished during the day, and what the results of those accomplishments were in terms of productivity. Your answer should indicate a high level of activity with a resultant high output of work of high quality.

13. "If you were hiring a person for a position similar to your last one, what traits would you look for?"

REALLY MEANS: "How do you perceive the requirements of your job?" In effect, the interviewer is asking you to describe yourself. If you were successful in your last job, go ahead and describe yourself, building on your strengths and playing down your weaknesses. For example, if your last job required a high degree of intelligence, a high energy level, outstanding interpersonal skills, strong technical competence, and day–to–day problem solving, then you should articulate those strengths.

14. "What do you know about opportunities in the field in which you are trained?"

REALLY MEANS: "How much knowledge and interest have you in your present career field?" Obviously, a vague, generalized answer to this question would indicate either that you haven't explored opportunities in your chosen career field or that you don't have enough interest and enthusiasm for your career field. In answering this question, be prepared to discuss all entry-level positions as well as top individuals in your chosen field.

15. "Have you had any serious illness or injury?"

REALLY MEANS: "If you had heart trouble, mental illness, or chronic alcoholism, it may be a knockout factor." Many companies are getting away from company physicals, due to government regulations that require and encourage employers to hire the handicapped. Often you'll encounter companies that have an enlightened position about giving individuals a fair chance in working for them. On the other hand, the personnel manager wants to hire the best person he or she can get for the job. If you've had a serious illness or injury that's now under control and you feel it won't give you recurring problems, you should try to minimize it in the interview. A candidate who goes into a great deal of explanation about a serious illness or injury is talking him- or herself out of a job. Employers are concerned that when they hire an individual to perform a job, that individual is capable of fulfilling requirements. If the individual hired can't perform the job, then the employer suffers a great loss. Carefully word any information you give out about your health, particularly if it's of a serious nature. I have had candidates tell me quite frankly that they had been alcoholics but that they were recovered. I appreciated very much hearing their sincerity and their honesty. However, in the final analysis, I had to make a decision about whether or not to take a chance on them. Invariably, I hired other candidates who didn't appear to have serious health problems.

16. *"What do you do to keep in good physical condition?"*

REALLY MEANS: "In order to perform efficiently and effectively, you must be in good physical shape." A candidate who keeps him- or herself fit has an edge over other candidates. If you don't engage in any physical conditioning programs or participate in any sports, then you should be prepared to come up with something that would indicate an effort on your part to stay physically fit, even if it only involves brisk walks. If, on the other hand, you engage in a lot of physical activity, then by all means tell the interviewer.

17. *"Are you willing to go where the company sends you?"*

REALLY MEANS: "How flexible are you?" If the interviewer does not have any specific geographic locations in mind, then you should answer this question in the affirmative. But follow it up by saying, "Yes, provided it is within a major metropolitan area," or whatever your preference happens to be. Do not indicate an unwillingness to relocate; it can only work against you. The time that it means something is when you're actually faced with the relocation; you can cross that bridge when you come to it. During the interview, however, play it smart and indicate that you're willing to relocate.

18. *"What single thing in your life would you judge to be your greatest achievement?"*

REALLY MEANS: "Are you an achiever?" Try to come up with something job related. If you can call to mind mastering a musical instrument or becoming a competition skier or diver or winning some award, then by all means relate that activity to the interviewer. The main thing, of course, is to indicate to the interviewer that you're capable of achieving noteworthy goals.

19. *"You have probably known some people who were (job title). What, in your opinion, are the chief causes of failure among them?"*
REALLY MEANS: "Have you ever looked at elements that lead to failure as well as the elements that lead to success?" The interviewer knows that the successful person has looked at both sides of the fence and has learned to maximize elements that lead to success and to reduce those elements that lead to failure.

Some causes of failure are:

1. Not meeting objectives
2. Producing a low volume of unacceptable work
3. Managing in such a way as not to obtain motivation and commitment among subordinates
4. Inhibiting subordinates from growing in their capacity to handle increasingly difficult work
5. Being unable to identify primary causes when faced with complex problems
6. Incorrectly zeroing in on the most essential aspects of a problem by being misled by secondary or irrelevant aspects
7. Inability to evaluate the probable consequences of an individual's actions
8. Inability to maintain relationships with others

In answering the question, think through items that you feel were the chief causes of failure among people you have known, then relate those to the interviewer in as clear and concise a manner as you can.

20. "What single skill or ability are you most expert at? How did you develop this expertise?"

REALLY MEANS: "Give me a succinct self-opinion." This question is subjective, and you should answer it as clearly and concisely as you can.

INDEX